THE
TIMELESS
SWING

THE TIMELESS SWING

TOM WATSON

WITH NICK SEITZ

PHOTOGRAPHS BY DOM FURORE

ATRIA BOOKS

NEW YORK   LONDON   TORONTO   SYDNEY

ATRIA B O O K S

A Division of Simon & Schuster, Inc.
1230 Avenue of the Americas
New York, NY 10020

First Atria Books hardcover edition March 2011

ATRIA B O O K S and colophon are trademarks of Simon & Schuster, Inc.

For information about special discounts for bulk purchases,
please contact Simon & Schuster Special Sales at
1-866-506-1949 or business@simonandschuster.com.

The Simon & Schuster Speakers Bureau can bring authors to your
live event. For more information or to book an event, contact the
Simon & Schuster Speakers Bureau at 1-866-248-3049 or visit our
website at www.simonspeakers.com.

Designed by Tim Oliver

Archival photographs courtesy of *Golf Digest*; photograph on page 208
by Tony Roberts, courtesy of Tom Watson

Video clips from the DVD *Tom Watson Lessons of a Lifetime*
courtesy of Tom Watson Productions

Manufactured in the United States of America

10   9   8   7   6   5   4   3   2   1

Library of Congress Cataloging-in-Publication Data

Watson, Tom, 1949–
   The timeless swing / Tom Watson with Nick Seitz.
      p. cm.
   1. Swing (Golf) I. Seitz, Nick, 1939– II. Title.
      GV979.S9W38 2011
      796.352'3—dc22

                                    2011000709

ISBN 978-1-4391-9483-6
ISBN 978-1-4391-9495-9 (ebook)

This book is dedicated to all the people who helped me learn . . .
and relearn . . . this wonderfully frustrating game.

I would especially like to mention Stan Thirsk, who took me under his wing
when I was eleven years old and throughout my life has continued to teach me not only
the correct ways of swinging the golf club, but more importantly how to live
one's life and treat people with grace and respect. Thank you, Stan.

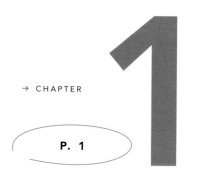

CONTENTS

**TOP OF
HIS GAME**
Tom Watson
has won eight
majors in
his brilliant
career.

FORE**WORD** BY JACK NICKLAUS

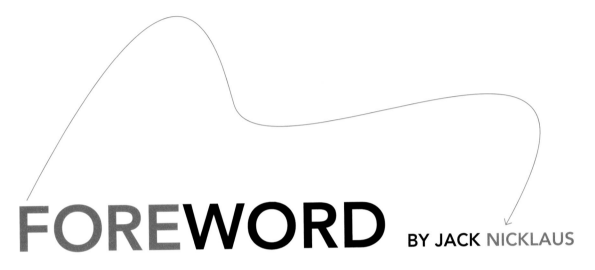

ANYONE WHO KNOWS ME can tell you that I am not exactly a "techie." But I am proud to say that in July 2009, I sent my very first text. Well, sort of. My wife, Barbara, actually sent it, but it was from my heart to her fingers. The message was to my good friend Tom Watson, who, only two months shy of his sixtieth birthday, was shocking the sports world with his run at a sixth British Open title. The text ended with, "Win one for us old guys, and make us all cry again."

We all know how the story ended, but nothing changed the chapters that got us to that dramatic moment. For one week, Tom Watson was anything but an "old

guy." He turned back the clock and turned heads by leading the Open after 72 holes. In the end, he was the victim of bad breaks, not bad decisions and certainly not bad golf. I was one of those who truly were not surprised by my friend's performance, because I long ago marveled at Tom's effortless, youthful, and, yes, timeless swing.

The first time I ever saw Tom swing a golf club was at an exhibition in Topeka, Kansas. Tom was just fifteen years old at the time, and while I don't remember a great deal from the day, I do remember a swing that spoke volumes about this young man's potential and promising future. Bridge that 45-year gap, and Tom's swing today is not too far removed from the one he first showed me in Topeka. It is the envy of every senior and a model for any junior.

Tom and I have played a great deal of golf together over the years. Some might have called us rivals, but only in the literal definition of the word. I would prefer to simply call us competitors. I would give Tom my best, and he always gave me his. In the 1977 Masters, the 1977 British Open, and the 1982 U.S. Open, I certainly gave Tom my best, but his was better. In the end, there was always a sincere handshake, an arm around the shoulder, and a great deal of mutual respect. Over the decades, that respect grew into a close friendship, and today we spend a lot of time together off the course, be it traveling together or fishing. On the course, I get the occasional benefit of being Tom's partner, and on more than one occasion, we've won one for us old guys.

In these pages, I hope you too can gain an appreciation for the man behind a swing that time has warmly embraced, and along the way learn a little something that can help you enjoy the game as much as my good friend Tom and I have over the years.

PRE**FACE** BY TOM WATSON

I AM WRITING THIS BOOK to pass along the best lessons I have learned during my golf career to help you improve and enjoy the game more. And to pay tribute to the different mentors, teachers, and players who have helped me so generously, starting with my late father. He was a keen student of the game and played it with a seriousness and passion I have rarely observed. He gave me the gift of never crediting any shot that wasn't struck just right.

I also owe thanks to great players and teachers like Jack Nicklaus, Byron Nelson, Sam Snead, Lee Trevino, Butch Harmon, David Leadbetter, and—most

Watson with mentor Stan Thirsk.

importantly—my lifelong friend and coach Stan Thirsk. I have learned about the swing from more people than I could ever think to credit, all the way back to Harry Vardon's thoughts on the grip.

I have taken these experts' thinking, along with my own observations and study, distilled it, and adapted what worked for me. That's the approach I commend to you using this book or any other golf instruction.

Everyone differs in strength, physique, and time to practice and play, but as I learned from Dad in my very first lesson, if you build a solid foundation of grip and setup, you can swing the club a lot of different ways and get playable results. Jack Nicklaus, during the many clinics I have hosted with him, has said it this way: "If you have the proper grip and proper setup, you can be taught."

I will show and describe to you my father's lessons and how they still apply today. I will show you how I swing the club and how I think it can apply to you, at any age level.

Ours is more and more the game of a lifetime. If you take care of yourself and concentrate on these few simple swing keys, it is my firm belief you will improve your ball striking.

I've always enjoyed playing with average golfers in pro-ams and friendly rounds at home, giving them pointers and seeing them get better. Doing this book with the help of my longtime friend and collaborator Nick Seitz, I found myself repeating and demonstrating a swing key that is seldom written or talked about: the vital need to meet the ball just before the bottom of the arc with virtually every shot.

I achieved real consistency in my ball striking only when I found the secret to my swing on tour, which I will explain in the book. I've continued to do it instinctively, but have never put it into words or pictures. It's a weakness in Nick's game as well as many other weekend golfers' games.

Your divots reveal a lot about your club/ball contact. The best divots I ever saw were Byron's divots: always consistently the same depth, width, and length . . . "dollar bills," as many people called them. He rarely hit the ball heavy, the way most of us do at least a little.

Simply by observing the shape and direction of your divots, you can get a good read on what the clubhead is doing at impact. Most golfers do not achieve a consistent contact/divot combination.

As I said in the beginning, all I want to accomplish with this book is to help you play better golf with the understanding that the fundamentals are just that—fundamental for consistent club/ball contact. Golf is a demanding game. No shortcuts. I hope you are ready to learn or relearn the basics that give you improvement and enjoyment.

INTRODUCTION BY NICK SEITZ

I'VE BEEN COLLABORATING ON instruction writing with Tom Watson for thirty years now, and been a grateful recipient of his swing advice. My grip will never be strong enough to suit him, but he persists. Boy, does he persist.

You get the feeling that he cares as much about your game as he cares about his own, and that he enjoys working and playing with average golfers as much as with tour players. He has gone overseas for The Open a week early to play links courses with old high-school pals from Kansas City. He relishes coaching his partners in pro-ams and corporate outings.

'WATSON'S QUEST FOR LEARNING AND IMPROVING IS

A strong traditionalist, he just plain loves all aspects of the game, from its earliest history to its latest techniques. As he grows older himself, he has developed a special feel for instruction that promotes longevity. If that doesn't make him unique among the great players, it makes him one of the rare few.

"The most amazing thing about him," says Jerry Tarde, the editor in chief of *Golf Digest*, "is that his interest in the instructional aspects of the game remains undimmed by the passage of time. As opposed to other superstars who either have a withering interest or never had much at all."

Watson's quest for learning and improving is never-ending, and his own swing reflects it. Leading teachers and players believe he is swinging better than he's ever swung.

On the practice range at a major championship not long ago, Padraig Harrington turned around to see whose shots were making such a crisp, pure sound. "I've never heard or seen a ball hit like that," Harrington marveled. It was Watson.

You no doubt are familiar with Watson's age-defying feats in recent years. He lost the 2009 British Open in a playoff at nearly sixty years of age and not long removed from hip replacement surgery, captivating the entire world of sports and a broader public as well.

In 2010 he hit the leaderboard in the early rounds of the Masters, made the cut, and finished under par in a tie for 18th place. Then he made the cut in the U.S. Open at Pebble Beach, where he won it in 1982, playing on a special exemption probably meant to be sentimental and ceremonial. Watson doesn't do sentimental and ceremonial.

He was paired for the first two rounds with young international stars Ryo Ishikawa of Japan and Rory McIlroy of Northern Ireland. Their ages combined didn't total his sixty. Watson finished 29th—ahead of both of them.

At one point over the weekend, a young man in the gallery shouted, "You rock, Tom Watson!"

It's fitting that Watson became the second golf professional emeritus at the five-star Greenbrier resort in West Virginia, succeeding the late Sam Snead. Snead could have given Old Man River two a side; he was the oldest man to win a PGA Tour title (at fifty-two) and contend in a major championship (third in the PGA Championship at sixty-two).

He is one of the role models Watson credits in this book. Both had long swings built to last and competitive fires that never needed stoking.

The lessons taught in this book have been developed over decades, but we're pleased to include a cutting-edge method for learning a few of them. In each chapter, you will see a Microsoft Tag. When you scan these Tags with your smartphone, you will be taken directly to a video of Tom Watson giving a demonstration of a lesson featured in that chapter of the book. These video clips make the reading experience more dynamic and also give a sample of Tom's instructional DVD from which they are drawn.

The first time you see one of these images, simply navigate your smartphone's browser to http://gettag.mobi to download the free app, then anytime you see:

 Point your smartphone's camera at it and enjoy the video.

NEVER-ENDING, **AND HIS OWN SWING REFLECTS IT.'**

So how does a legendary golfer produce a book like this? How much does Watson really get involved? Here's a snapshot of the process. He and I and Dom Furore, a top golf photographer, get together for a week at a golf course, in this case the Greenbrier. I know that sounds enviable, but consider that the work days began at dawn and didn't end till dusk.

Watson demonstrates a topic, Dom photographs it digitally, I capture Watson's commentary on a tape recorder. Afterward the recording is transcribed with copies for Watson and me, and Dom prints the photos. Watson picks the best pictures, often making notes on the proof sheets to suggest graphic highlighting. Watson and I go back and forth until we're satisfied with the text, then we both review the finished layouts. He could not be more involved in the entire process, start to finish.

A word of explanation to our left-handed and/or lady golfing friends. We realize that the accepted language of the game isn't ideal, intended as it is for right-handed, male players. Over the years, leading publications like *Golf Digest* have experimented with "neutral" references that seemed forced and unnatural, and caused more confusion for most people than the usual terminology. We hope you will make the conversions that may well have become second nature by now.

And I hope Watson's swing advice helps you as much as it has helped me over the golfing years. May there be many more for all of us. It's not called the game of a lifetime frivolously.

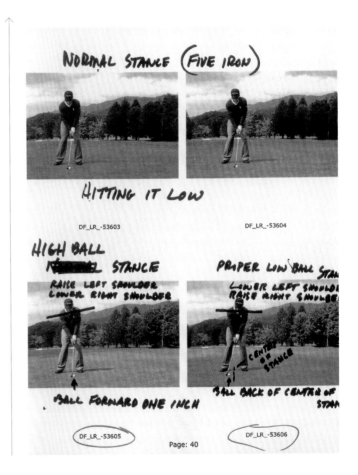

→ **KEY CONCEPTS**

'EVERY GOLFER SHOULD BE STRIVING FOR A CONSISTENT BOTTOM OF THE ARC ON EVERY SWING.'

1

1

KEY CONCEPTS

I WANT TO BE VERY SURE YOU UNDERSTAND right at the outset two crucial concepts that we will revisit throughout this book: the bottom of the arc and the spine angle. I want to introduce and define them in this opening section. Later I will show you how I find the bottom of the arc and practice to produce it consistently, and how I check my spine angle and you can too. They are absolutely critical to every golf swing. I don't find them stressed enough in golf instruction, especially the bottom of the arc. And I fear it shows in the average golfer's difficulty improving.

BOTTOM OF THE ARC

The golf swing is a circular motion or an arc. For most shots, contact should be made just before the club reaches the bottom of the arc (yellow arrow indicates the bottom of the arc). Most people hit the ball fat or thin instead.

SPINE ANGLE

A golfer creates a spine angle when he bends forward from the waist, keeping his back straight and flexing the knees. The upper body turns around this spine angle both back and through. The spine angle is an axis to swing around. *It should not change from address through impact.*

THE BOTTOM OF THE ARC

THE GOLF swing is an arc, and the lowest part of the swing is referred to as the bottom of the arc. Everything we will talk about in this book is geared to producing a consistent bottom of the arc in the swing. It is a much misunderstood concept.

Johnny Miller believes it's the most important lesson you can learn to develop a good swing. He taught it in a clinic and exhibition I did with him and Arnie and Jack not long ago. I like it that we agree on this key point.

Every golfer should be striving for a consistent bottom of the arc *on every swing*. It's the most important element in a repeatable swing. It applies to almost every iron shot you play off turf (the driver and putter are struck slightly on the upswing). When we hit the ball "fat" (the divot starts before the ball) or "thin" (the club hits too high on the ball) we are not finding a consistent bottom of the arc.

It's a major difference between pros and most amateurs. The pros make "ball-divot contact," as Eddie Merrins calls it in his teaching. The bottom of the arc is *ahead of the ball*. A lot of poorer players hit the turf before the ball or are otherwise inconsistent reaching the bottom of the arc—that's mainly why they're poorer players.

We can fix that if you absorb the lessons in this book.

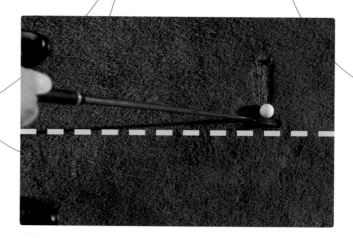

The tee marks the bottom of the arc—ahead of the ball—for a typical iron swing. Here it's a 5-iron.

FIND THE BOTTOM OF YOUR ARC

HERE'S HOW I practice hitting iron shots off the turf. I draw a line out from the middle of my stance as shown. I put a ball down on that line, and I want my divot to start at the forward edge of the line. The bottom of the arc occurs well in front of the line, not *on* the line and definitely not *behind* the line. The bottom of the arc is ahead of the center of my stance.

I'm using a 5-iron here, with my normal ball position for that club. Your ball position for a particular club might be slightly forward or behind the middle of your stance. I vary my ball position from the middle of my stance for different irons, slightly forward for the long irons and slightly behind for the short irons—but not more than a couple inches off center.

Byron Nelson was the best divot taker I've ever seen. His divots were as square, as shallow, and as long as anybody could ever take. They resembled a dollar bill and extended several inches through the ball. Byron rarely hit the ball heavy the way most of us do at least a bit.

On the course, you determine the bottom of your arc with your practice swings. Most people make practice swings they don't repeat with their real swings. And I see a lot of amateurs make a poor weight transfer and fail to get the club to the ball before they take a divot. The bottom of the arc for them is behind the ball instead of ahead of it.

If you've shifted your weight on the downswing, your right knee should be pointing toward the ball at impact. If you haven't shifted your weight—and you hit off your right foot—the bottom of your arc will be behind the ball. You'll probably hit it out to the right.

SPINE ANGLE

THE SPINE angle is an axis to swing around. It should not change from address, to the top of the swing, and down through impact.

If you can achieve a consistent spine angle, a lot of good things will happen. To name just one, your swing path will be good.

You establish your spine angle simply by standing up straight, then bending from the waist and flexing your knees. The angle of your upper body should not be at all slumped. We'll deal further with posture in chapter 2.

A sound spine angle stabilizes you and keeps your head from bobbing up and down. A little sideways movement is okay if your spine angle is consistent.

Watch Tom Watson giving a demonstration of one of the lessons featured within this chapter. Go to http://gettag .mobi for your free mobile app, then point your smart- phone's camera at the Microsoft Tag and enjoy the video.

8

'YOUR HANDS CONNECT YOU TO THE CLUB. YOU MUST PUT THEM ON THE CLUB CORRECTLY.'

→ **PRE-SWING BASICS**

11

PRE-SWING BASICS

JACK NICKLAUS ONCE SAID, "If you have the proper grip and proper set-up, you can be taught." I wholeheartedly agree—and would expand his comment to include ALL the fundamentals we are going to talk about. Golf fans think the tour pros are on the practice range sharing secret insights to the swing and working on esoteric keys to which they, average golfers, are not privy. They'd love to listen in. Well, I'm afraid we're not hiding anything so intriguing or revolutionary. We're out there working on tried and proven fundamentals, by the hour. When our games go off, the cause almost always is a lapse in our fundamentals. We might be standing a little too far from the ball, or our grips have slipped back into old bad habits. We practice the fundamentals, and enjoy it. Nothing ever beats the kick you get from a cleanly struck golf shot!

1. VARDON OVERLAPPING GRIP
Named after the legendary Harry Vardon, who won the British Open six times. This is the grip I use. The little finger of the right hand overlaps the left hand in the indentation between the left index finger and middle finger. The nine fingers on the club form a cohesive unit.

THE THREE BASIC GRIPS

THE GRIP may not be the most exciting fundamental to many of you—but it's the most important. A good swing starts with a good grip. A bad swing starts with a poor grip.

I would say that 95 percent of the leisure golfers I see lack a sound grip. They'll never be able to play to their potential or even close to it.

We'll look at the three most popular grips: the Vardon overlapping grip, the interlocking grip, and the 10-finger grip. I use the Vardon grip because I feel the ring finger of the right hand is positioned better, allowing for better wrist hinging. The Vardon grip unifies the hands and helps them work together.

2. THE INTERLOCKING GRIP The little finger of the right hand interweaves with the index finger of the left hand. Jack Nicklaus and Tiger Woods use this one. Jack believes it's the most natural, solid grip.

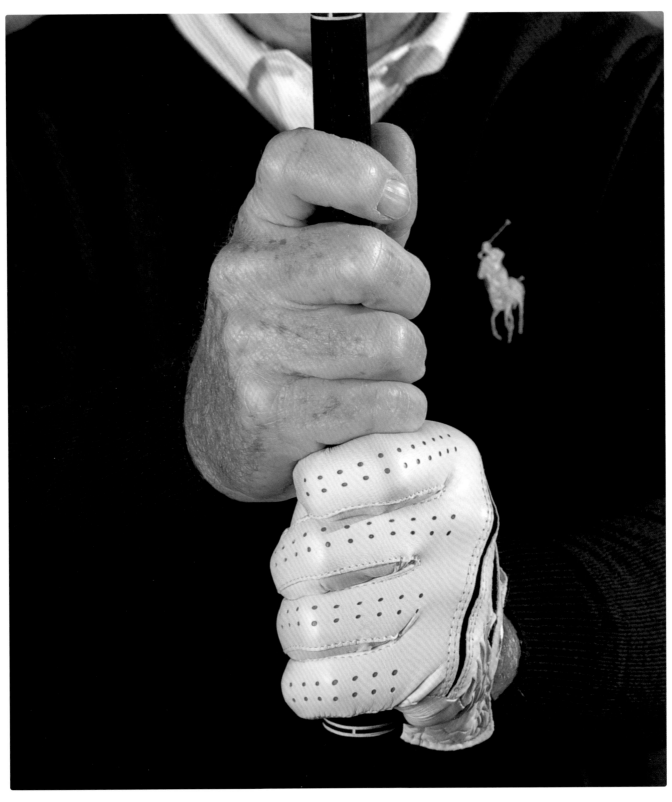

3. THE 10-FINGER GRIP Also called the baseball grip. All 10 fingers are on the club.
Its proponents believe it promotes easier wrist action, for one thing.

'GRIP THE CLUB MAINLY IN YOUR FINGERS INSTEAD OF YOUR PALMS.'

MY GRIP ADVICE

Your hands connect you to the club. You must put them on the club correctly. I would like to see you grip the club mainly with your fingers instead of your palms. Your fingers give you feel. If you reach into your pocket to pull out a coin, you feel it with your fingers. Also, you grip more lightly with your fingers than your palms. With a good grip, you can whip the clubhead through the ball faster, which means more distance.

In a proper grip, the *left* hand goes on first. When I was six years old, my dad put my hands on the club and the first thing he said was, "Son, turn that left hand over so you see two knuckles."

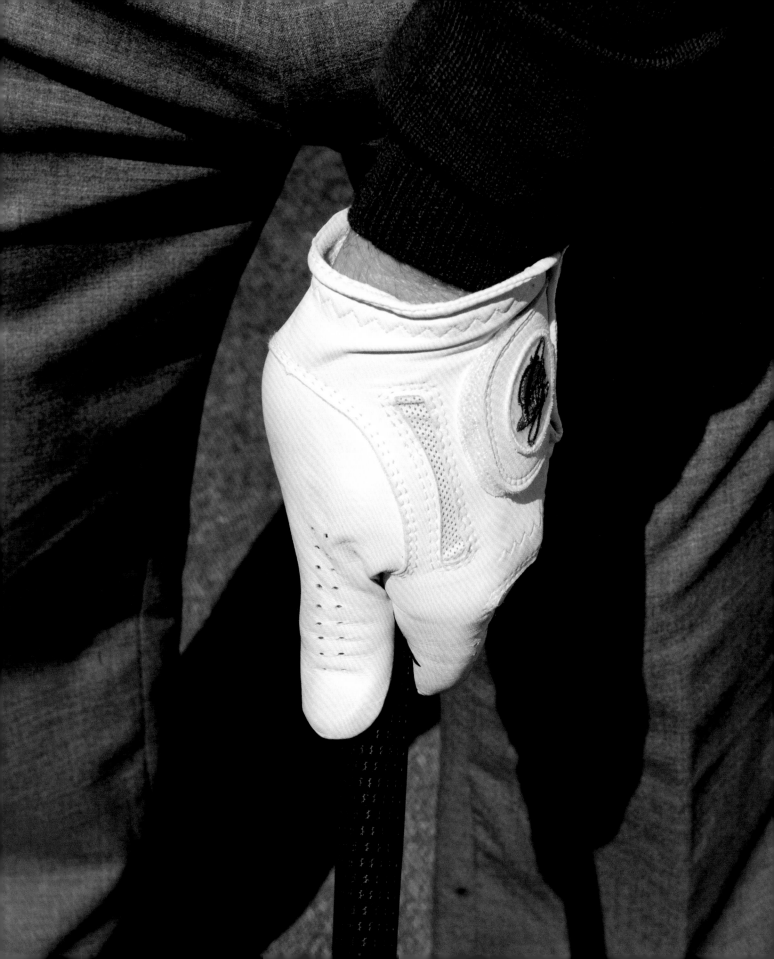

MY GRIP ADVICE

The left thumb goes down the right center of the shaft—NOT on top. The right thumb goes down the left side of the shaft. The pad of the right thumb fits over the top of the left thumb. Point the "V's" formed between your thumbs and index fingers at your right shoulder. Note that the lifeline of the right hand overlaps the thumb of my left hand. You want to leave a slight space between the forefinger and middle finger of your right hand. That allows you to cradle the club without gripping too tightly.

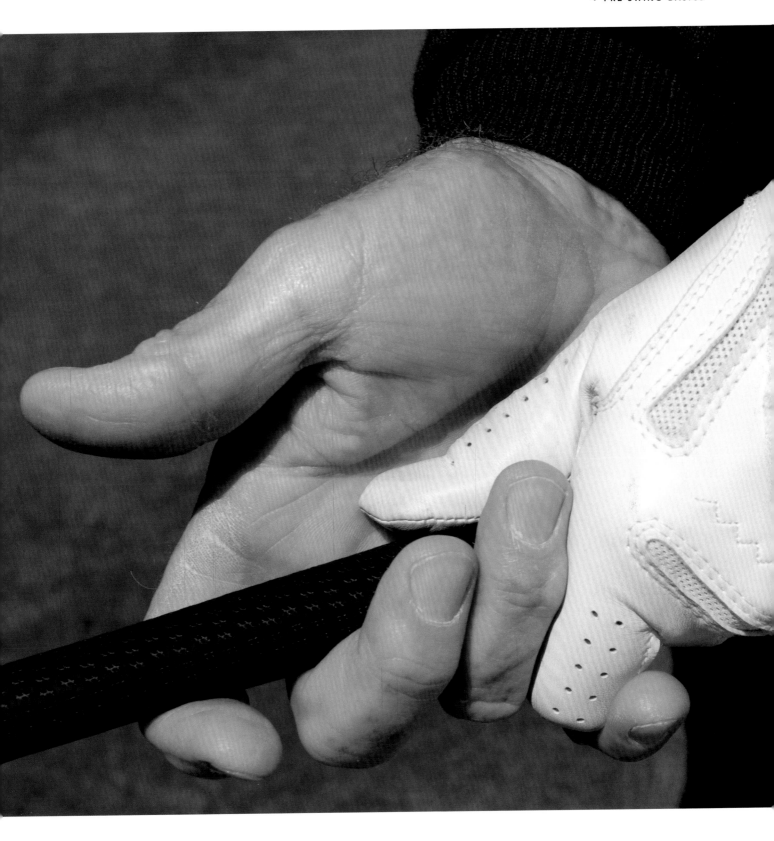

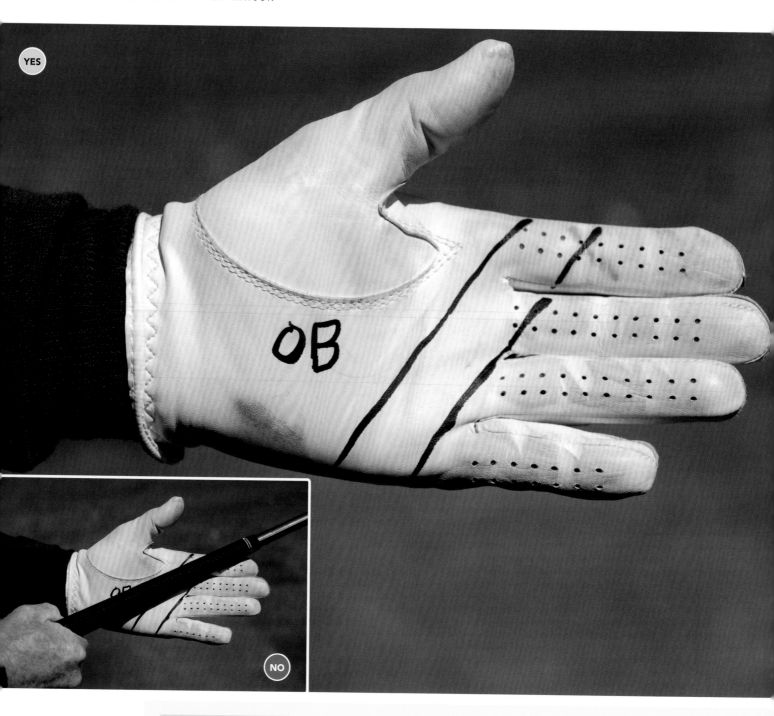

YES

NO

A WAY TO LEARN IT

My great friend and teacher Stan Thirsk does this with his pupils: He takes the glove and draws two lines on it, and also draws the letters OB, standing for out-of-bounds. He wants them to lay the club in the left hand between the two lines—not in the OB or palm area.

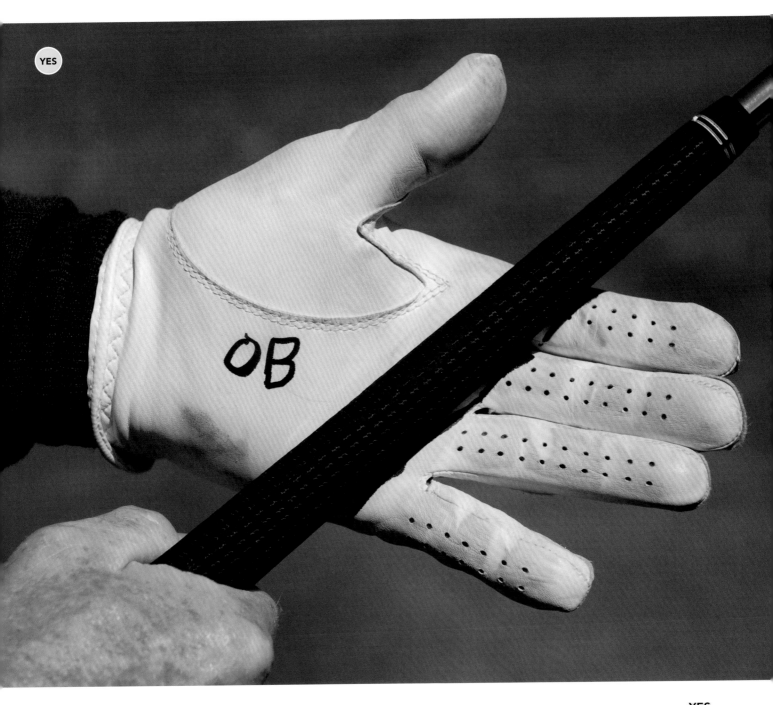

YES

YES
The club lies in the fingers of *the left hand* and runs across the ring and middle fingers, cleanly against the index finger.

Watch Tom Watson giving a demonstration of one of the lessons featured within this chapter. Go to http://gettag.mobi for your free mobile app, then point your smartphone's camera at the Microsoft Tag and enjoy the video.

A WAY TO LEARN IT

Try this connect-the-dots test to see if your hands are connecting properly on the club.

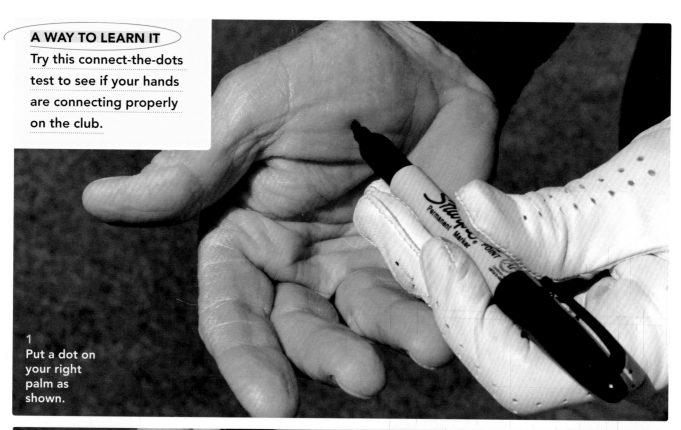

1
Put a dot on your right palm as shown.

2
Put another dot on your left thumb.

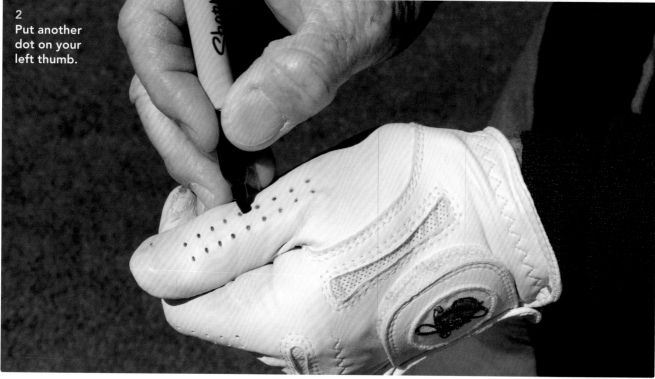

3
Connect the dots on your hand and glove. You have your well-assembled grip.

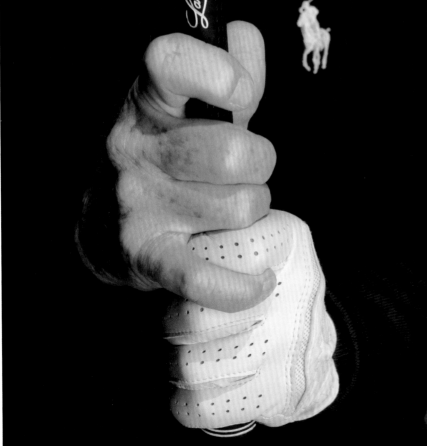

REVIEW

→ **Left hand** on club, seeing two knuckles.

→ **Left thumb** down right center of shaft, "V" pointed at right shoulder.

→ **Right hand** on club with pad of right thumb over left thumb, "V" pointed at right shoulder.

→ **Split** right forefinger and middle finger.

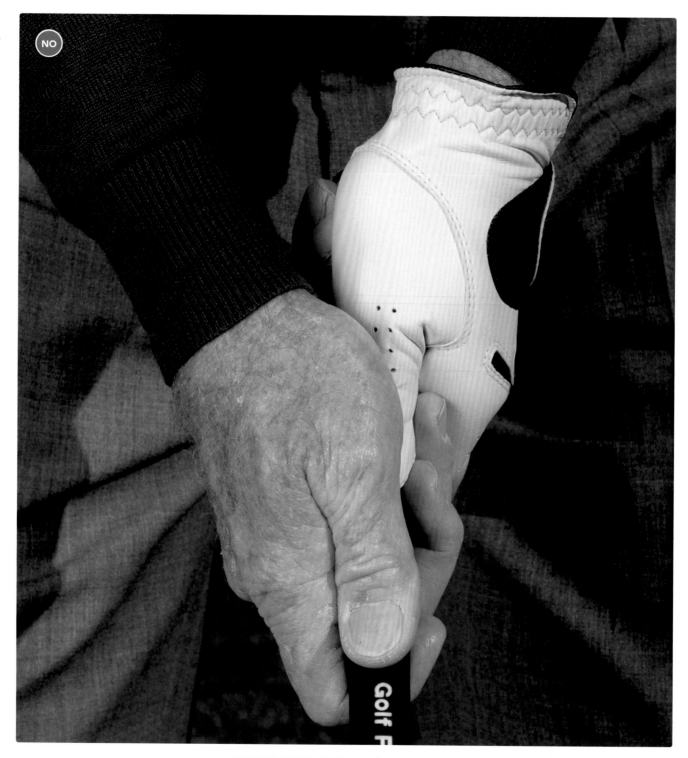

NO

COMMON FAULTS

GRIP TOO WEAK This is the mistake I see most. Too many people put the left thumb and right thumb straight down the top of the shaft. That inhibits their wrist break and hand/clubhead speed. The clubface opens, causing a slice.

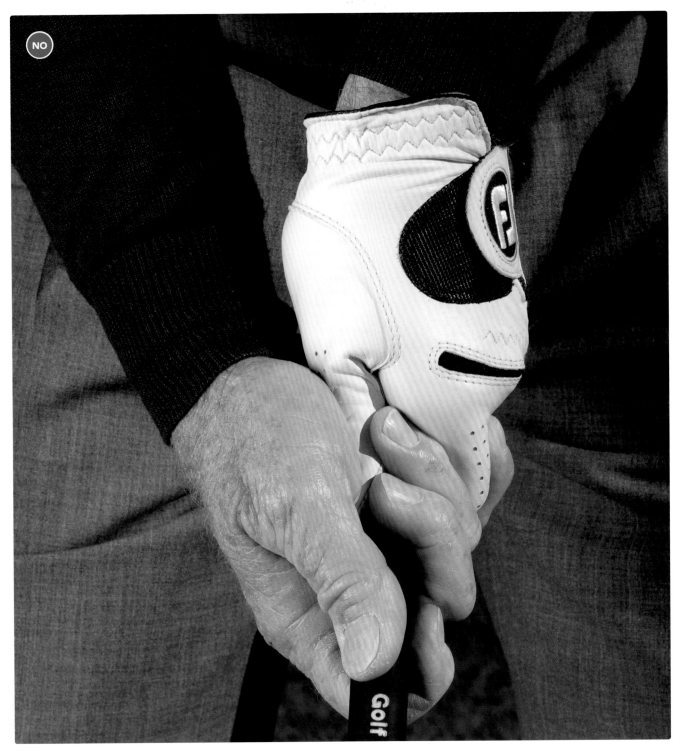

GRIP TOO STRONG Conversely, if you see too many knuckles on the left hand, the club-face probably will close at impact and cause a hook. Still, a strong grip is a power position. I would rather see your grip too strong than too weak, especially if you're a slicer.

1

2

3

GRIP PRESSURE

You've learned the proper grip. Now the question becomes "How firmly do you hold the club?" Essentially a golfer needs just enough grip pressure to control the club. You have to grip firmly, but not so firmly that you create tension in your forearms. The forearms have to be relaxed and active to make a good swing.

If your grip pressure is good, you will be able to swing rhythmically. Your mechanics will blend together smoothly, and you will be able to feel where the clubhead is during the swing. The common tendency is to grip too tightly, but generally, lighter is better than tighter.

How do you determine your best grip pressure?

President Gerald Ford once asked me how to determine the ideal grip pressure. Here's the approach I gave him.

Grip a club and point it straight up in the air in front of you, where it feels lightest (1). Let the club slide down through your hands (2, 3). Regrip the club and point it up in the air again, but this time reduce your grip pressure to just enough to keep it from sliding through your hands (4). Extend it horizontally in front of you (5). That's as much grip pressure as you need to hit the ball. You'll be amazed how lightly you can hold the club and control it, as well as how much more freely you can swing it.

4

5

HOW TO PRACTICE

When you practice, loosen your grip pressure—back off until the club is almost falling out of your hands. Start with the lightest possible pressure, then gradually firm it up until you can control the club without it slipping at all in your hands. You probably have found your best grip pressure. I would bet it's not as tight as before.

'YOU'LL BE AMAZED HOW LIGHTLY YOU CAN HOLD THE CLUB AND CONTROL IT.'

LEFT HAND

PRESSURE POINTS

By following this approach, you will feel a natural increase in grip pressure in the last three fingers of your left hand and the middle two fingers of your right hand. Ben Hogan talked about these being the pressure points in the grip. I stress the same thing.

I apply most of the gripping pressure with the last three fingers of my left hand—as much pressure as I can without causing my left arm to tighten—especially the little finger, which I consider the most vital pressure point for a good, firm grip. Try taking it off the club and see how well you can support the club.

Essentially the left hand is on the club to guide it, with the right hand supplying touch and power. That's why the left hand should grip the club more firmly than the right. If I keep my left hand solidly on the club, I won't lose it during the swing.

I apply just enough pressure with the right hand

RIGHT HAND

to keep the club from slipping in my hands and to unify the two hands during the swing. (If you develop blisters, the club is slipping.) Virtually no pressure should come from the right thumb and forefinger.

Hogan would leave his right thumb and forefinger off the club when he practiced.

I played guard in high school and got in this balanced position when I was on defense. I was ready to move quickly. At Stanford, I stuck to golf.

THE SETUP

WHEN I set up to the ball, I think of a basketball player in the guarding position. If he's in a good, ready position, he can move side to side or forward and backward, and stay in balance. He has to be on the balls of his feet with his knees flexed and his feet about shoulder-width apart.

I see a lot of poor posture when I play with average golfers. If your feet are too far apart, you can't shift your weight well. Feet too close together, you lose your balance. Legs too straight, you can't move at all. I see all those stances. I can almost always predict when my higher-handicap friends are going to hit a good shot. Their posture will be good, and posture pretty much dictates how you will hit the ball.

LEARN TO SET UP

Try this 1-2-3-4 approach to setting up.

1. Stand up straight, with your feet shoulder-width apart. Your feet are slightly open, the left toe a little more open than the right. That's so you can turn your lower body more easily through impact. Your right shoulder is slightly lower than your left, making it easier to grip the club.

2. Bend from the waist to form a straight spine angle that you want to keep throughout the swing. No slumping in the back!

3. Flex your knees slightly, and kick your right knee in toward your left knee to help brace on the inside of your right foot on the backswing.

4. Now stick your rear end out, until you feel a little tension in the small of your back. You're counter-balancing your top half being bent over.

I see too many people with their rear ends tucked in and their shoulders slumped. Make sure your rear end sticks out and your back is straight.

Your neck is an extension of your spine. Keep your chin up and your spine angle straight. Don't let your head slump, or you'll restrict your backswing.

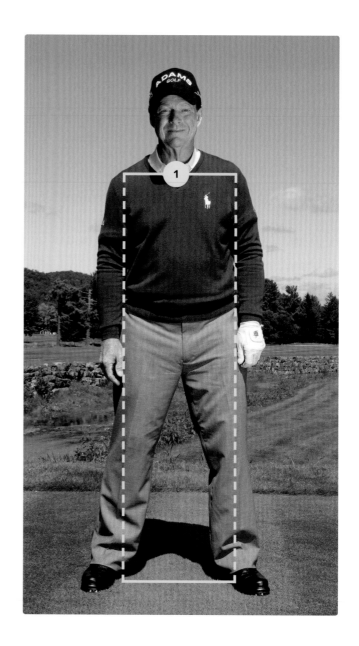

A GOOD SETUP

You're on the balls of your feet—not the heels, not the toes, THE BALLS OF YOUR FEET. That's the key to balance. No good athlete in any sport plays with his weight back on his heels. There's a good reason for that.

YES

YES

YES

YES

YES

REVIEW

→ **Bend** from waist.

→ **Back** straight.

→ **Rear end** out.

→ **Weight** on balls of feet.

YES

HOW FAR TO STAND FROM THE BALL

"How far do I stand from the ball?"

I get this question a lot. I see people all the time reaching for the ball with their arms extended stiffly, tensing their shoulders. It's a common cause of slicing. You should never feel you have to reach for the ball, even with a driver. You shouldn't feel cramped either, but I see reaching much more often.

HOW FAR TO STAND FROM THE BALL

Do you ever see a top PGA Tour pro extend his arms at address? Let your arms hang.

Without a club, start in the balanced posture we just talked about. Allow your arms to hang freely, then bring your hands together. That's where you grip the golf club. You should be looking *in* at your hands, not out at them. Finally, grip a club, move into the ball, and you're ready to hit the shot.

The distance you stand from the ball will automatically change depending on the length of the club. The longer the club, the farther you'll stand from the ball. Your posture doesn't change from club to club.

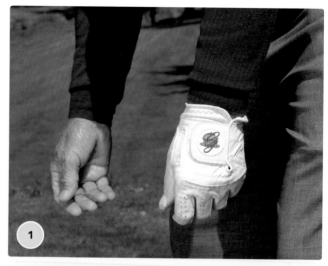

STANCE
LINE

AIM
LINE

TARGET
LINE

AIM AND ALIGNMENT

AIM AND alignment have a lot to do with where your shot will go. Like the other pre-swing fundamentals, these are factors you can control.

The proper sequence is: *You aim the clubface, then align your body.* In that order.

If you can hit a perfectly straight shot, with no wind affecting it, then your starting imaginary target line would run straight from the ball to your target. You would align your feet, knees, hips, and shoulders *parallel to that target line*, not at the target itself. This is the biggest difference I see in amateurs compared to pros. Amateurs align the body at the target instead of *parallel* to the target line.

But straight shots are rare in this game. The wind and your natural ball flight—a slice or a hook—make the ball move left or right away from the direction you start the ball. Most shots have some sort of curve to them—from your natural fade or draw, or from a crosswind.

When we talk about the aim line, we're talking about the line we want to immediately *start* the ball on. So we have to adjust our aim line and body alignment to allow for the bend of the ball in the air and its bounce when it hits the ground. I have a natural right-to-left draw or hook swing, so I want to allow for the ball starting to the right and then curving back to my target in the fairway or on the green.

I do that by moving my aim line and my parallel body alignment slightly to the right. If your basic shot shape is left to right, you need to move your aim line and body alignment to the left.

As I said, a common fault of average golfers is aligning the body at the target, often because they walk up to the ball and align their bodies before they aim the clubface. Think about it. If your body is aligned at the target, your clubface is almost surely aimed to the right of the target. Most amateurs aim too far to the right. Then they naturally swing down left, across their bodies, to get the ball on line— which only aggravates their slices.

Your body should be aligned "parallel left" of your aim line. That way, the clubface can be easily squared to the aim line. Then you don't have to make compensations in your swing to pull or push the club through the impact zone.

REVIEW

→ **Determine** how much you think your ball will curve or drift from the start of its flight.

→ **Aim** the clubface square to this aim line.

→ **Then** align body to aim line.

THE NICKLAUS METHOD

Jack was known for this method on tour. He follows it meticulously. Although I don't usually use it myself, I do recommend it as the best way for most other golfers, including beginners and players who tend to spray their shots.

Jack stands behind the ball to determine his aim line and then picks a spot a foot or two in front of the ball on this intended aim line. The spot he focuses on might be a leaf or a different-colored bit of grass. He looks at that spot and through it to his target. Then he aligns his body parallel to this aim line.

As he walks into his stance, he keeps looking at this spot. He sets the club down and aims the clubface at the spot. Taking his stance, square to his aim line, he then looks up at his target. He swivels his head to look at the spot, and then at the target. Again, he looks at the spot, looks at the target. One last look at his spot for confirmation and he starts his swing. This is the best way to aim and align yourself.

I might add that using this sort of pre-shot routine can keep you from being subconsciously influenced by a tee box or tee markers pointing you off line. If you're not careful, angled tee boxes and/or markers can cost you accuracy. Even mowing stripes can encourage you to aim in a direction you don't want to go.

NICKLAUS 1
Jack aims the clubhead
at his intermediate
spot (second ball, in
the foreground) . . .

NICKLAUS 2
. . . looks at his
intermediate
spot . . .

NICKLAUS 3
. . . looks at his target . . . then repeats steps 2 and 3, and starts his swing.

THE WATSON METHOD

Another way to aim and align (the way I do it) is to visualize football goalposts in the fairway or on the green. The two posts represent right and left limits for my shot. On a tee shot those limits might span the entire fairway—and even the rough if it poses no serious problem. Or it might span only a quarter of the fairway. And some of the rough.

I set my limits to suit my usual shot shape, and then I factor in the wind. I want to leave myself the best angle for my next shot.

If I'm hitting my usual slight draw, I'll favor a target area from the right goalpost over to the center of the opening between the posts to "make a field goal," rather than pick an exact point to aim at. If the wind is blowing from left to right, I'll favor the left post to the center.

I give myself a width to hit to versus picking an exact point. Sometimes that makes it easier to hit a fairway or green. If I hit my right or left limit, I'm still in the fairway or on the green.

All you slicers should aim more carefully than what I often see. On a dogleg left with a fairway bunker at the left corner, the first thing you should do is tee up on the far right side of the tee box. Your left limit or goalpost should be the left edge of the bunker, or even left of that if there's a slice wind. Your right limit would be the middle of the fairway.

You shouldn't shy away from aiming at the bunker if you slice consistently. Your drive will probably wind up in the middle of the fairway, and you'll shorten the hole.

'I GIVE MYSELF A WIDTH TO HIT TO VERSUS PICKING AN EXACT POINT.'

PW   5-i   D

BALL POSITION

THERE ARE two theories about positioning the ball in your stance.

Some golfers subscribe to the theory that the ball should be in the same place for every club in the bag. Driver through wedges—all just forward of center.

Others, like me, subscribe to the theory that ball position should vary with the club—forward for longer clubs and back toward the middle with shorter clubs. The reason is that the bottom of the arc moves with the club.

My hitting zone is from the middle of my stance forward. The longer the club, the farther forward I play the ball. For a normal shot with a driver, that's opposite my left heel. For a 5-iron it's a little ahead of center. For a wedge it's center.

Remember the importance of finding the bottom of the arc. Everything we do with our swings we do to produce a consistent bottom of the arc. If you know where that is, your ball position can follow. The bottom of the arc, remember, is just *before*

51

reaching the ball with the driver, and just *after* reaching the ball with the irons (ball-divot).

Ball position is much misunderstood, and if you get it wrong it's nearly impossible to hit a good shot. Frequently I see people who slice the ball with the driver—but position the ball so far forward, or left in their stance, that they can never hit it solidly. Or the ball is so far back in the stance that they aim out to the right. With the irons, they mostly hit behind the ball.

Tour pros pay a lot more attention to ball position than most of you do. Still, faulty ball position often is the culprit behind a pro's problems. If we position the ball too far forward in the stance, we tend to move too much to reach it; if it's too far back, our body movement forward is restricted and we're prone to throw the club at the ball.

Remember, the ball should be positioned just before the bottom of your swing arc for most shots. If you know where the bottom of the arc is, you know where to position the ball. You can find the bottom with practice swings.

WARNING: Many golfers make careless practice swings that don't mirror their real swings. Don't make that mistake: Your practice swings need to mimic your real swings.

REVIEW
→ **Ball position** changes with different clubs.

→ **Remember** the bottom of the arc.

→ **Make** realistic practice swings.

WATSON MOMENT

*S*AM AT AUGUSTA

I REMEMBERED Sam Snead's advice about a steady head when I came to the par-3 16th hole in the 1977 Masters. The last day I was tied for the lead with Jack Nicklaus. As I swung a 5-iron, I had that one thing in mind: keep my head still and swing my shoulders around it. I hit the shot dead-center flush, right at the flag. The pressure I'd been feeling all day just drained out of my body, replaced by the confidence I felt from performing that shot in such a crucial situation. I two-putted for par, birdied 17, and parred 18 to win.

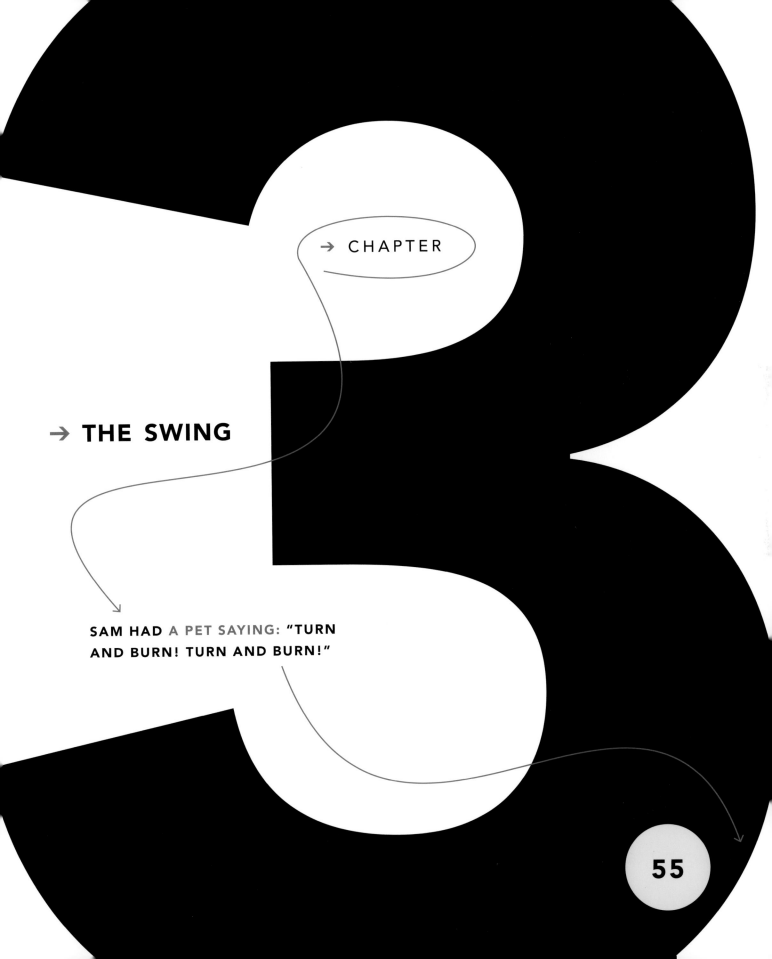

→ CHAPTER

→ **THE SWING**

SAM HAD A PET SAYING: "TURN AND BURN! TURN AND BURN!"

55

3

THE SWING

WE'VE COVERED THE ALL-IMPORTANT FUNDAMENTALS that form the foundation of the swing. Now it's time to get to the action and swing the club, from takeaway through to a balanced finish. I'll give you my keys to each stage of the swing, and show and tell you how I check myself at these different stages. Then we'll pull the parts together into a cohesive, rhythmic whole that forms the complete swing. Sam Snead was my dad's picture of a perfect swing with rhythm and power. I was fortunate to play golf with and be around Sam on Tour and at the Greenbrier resort. We often talked about how to swing the golf club. He understood the swing and what made it work, especially his own swing. And he was an entertaining and effective teacher for a long, long time, even if he never got much credit for it. I owe him a lot for the knowledge I received.

FIND YOUR
WAGGLE

I BELIEVE in leading into the takeaway by staying in motion with the feet, waggling the club and making a forward press.

Some modern tour players start the backswing from a stationary position at address. I still think having something in motion is important to avoid tension and establish the tempo and path for the swing.

Starting from a static club position at address can cause your grip pressure to change when the heat's on, and that isn't good, even if the change is slight. If a stationary start works for you, fine. For most of you I suggest two ways you can start from motion.

→ Feel the weight of the clubhead with your waggle. That helps keep your grip pressure light.

Or you can do what Mike Weir does and actually preview your backswing by swinging the club back to waist high as you would in your real swing.

Personally, I waggle the club back and forth from the ball a couple times, letting my hands and wrists hinge a little to relax them. (I pick the club up over the ball before I waggle, but that's just a habit; I'd prefer to waggle low and along the line of my takeaway.) I rock a bit from my right foot to my left foot with each of my two waggles.

Think of the waggle as a way to relax under pressure. Develop your own routine for getting into the swing—but stay in motion.

Players advanced enough to curve their shots intentionally can try adjusting their waggles to maneuver the ball from left to right or right to left. Normally the club path will be straight back from the ball for the first foot or two. To hook the ball, you want to swing the club back somewhat inside your normal path, so waggle to the inside. To slice, swing the club more outside, so waggle more outside. Most of you, as slicers, want to avoid the latter approach.

REVIEW

→ **Start** in motion.
→ **Feel** the clubhead.
→ **Keep** grip pressure light.
→ **Develop** your own routine.

ADDRESS

LIFT UP

HINGE BACK

RETURN

THE FORWARD PRESS

YOU CAN use what's called a forward press to make a smooth transition from your waggle into your takeaway. The forward press goes back to the days of hickory shafts, and was carried on into the age of modern shafts. It precedes backswings on tour in various forms.

At the end of my waggling, I forward press before I start my backswing by kicking my right knee in slightly toward my left knee. Then I smoothly start my left arm away from the ball. It's a starter, the way a car has a starter. Gary Player has always had a conspicuous forward press, with his right knee kicking toward the ball. This mirrors his lower-body impact position.

Sam Snead and Jack Nicklaus always swiveled their heads around to their right, which encourages a free shoulder turn.

Consistency is the thing. These great players performed the same mannerisms prior to starting every swing, which helped them move smoothly and confidently into their takeaways.

YES

LAST THOUGHT
BEFORE SWINGING

MY LAST thought before I swing is a rhythm thought. Not anything mechanical.

I want the club to swing like a pendulum. A pendulum goes back smoothly, changes direction smoothly, goes forward smoothly.

I want to swing every club at the same easy pace, from driver down to wedge. Long clubs take a little more time to swing, but your tempo should not change and get faster or slower. Most weekend players speed up their swings with the longer clubs, and have trouble making solid contact on the sweet spot. That costs them both distance and accuracy. Learn to recognize when your rhythm is too fast, and slow it down.

Another good rhythm image is to picture in your mind a player whose tempo you admire. It might be a tour player like Ernie Els or a good player at the course where you play.

My natural rhythm is fast, but it still needs to be consistent. I'm always conscious of that.

The first couple feet of your backswing pretty much determine your rhythm. All the more reason to make your last thought a rhythm thought.

THE TAKEAWAY

WE'LL PROCEED to break down the swing into its main parts, always keeping in mind that it's a *flowing* motion that adds up to more than the sum of these parts. When I was a youngster, I read an article where Arnold Palmer said that the first two feet of the backswing are the most important part of the swing. I believe it.

The first two feet establish your tempo and swing path. After that, you have little time to make an adjustment for an incorrect takeaway. That's why it's so critical to execute your takeaway well and consistently.

Think of taking the club away from the ball with the left hand, left forearm, and left shoulder staying in the same relative position they started in at address. I want a feeling of "togetherness" as my left hand, arm, and shoulder swing back in one piece until the clubhead is past my right foot. The right hand is just along for the ride.

A lot of average golfers immediately start hinging their wrists at the start of their backswing. When you overuse the hands on the takeaway, you narrow the width of the arc of the swing, causing an early unhinging of the wrists on the downswing. The club can set too early in the swing, or it can unleash too early—a lot of things can go wrong.

At the other extreme, holding the address position too long into the backswing prevents the right arm from folding properly.

When you swing the club back properly for the first two feet, with the left hand, arm, and shoulder moving in unison, the weight of the club will cause the wrists to start breaking once the clubhead passes the rear foot.

Ernie Els is a perfect modern example of this classic one-piece takeaway.

A key checkpoint is that *the hands are in, the clubhead out*. You're maintaining the angle formed by your left arm and the clubshaft at address. You don't want to break that angle too soon during the takeaway. The hands remain passive until the clubhead passes the back foot. There the clubhead is outside the hands because the angle between the left arm and the clubshaft has not changed. The hands and wrists start to hinge *past* this point, *not before*.

They will naturally hinge to the top of the swing, into a proper position. The left thumb is under the shaft. The club will feel light. But if you rotate the *clubhead* in and the *hands* out, the club gets laid off and feels heavy, and at the top the left thumb is on the side of the shaft rather than under it (see photos).

Another ingredient to a proper takeaway is your tempo. I have a pretty fast takeaway. Fred Couples, on the other hand, takes it away nice and slowly. You must swing with your own natural rhythm.

It's possible to take the club away too slowly— but almost no one does. Most of us need to slow down on the takeaway. That will improve the overall rhythm of your swing.

REVIEW
→ **The first two feet** are crucial.

→ **Left hand, arm, and shoulder** move together.

→ **Maintain address angle** between shaft and left arm.

→ **Find** your own tempo.

HANDS IN, CLUBHEAD OUT

HANDS OUT, CLUBHEAD IN

THE BACKSWING

YOUR LEFT shoulder, arm, and hand start the backswing in unison, as we've said. The left knee begins to fold or collapse in toward the ball, with the right hip turning back out of the way. This helps you maintain a consistent spine angle throughout the backswing. I learned as a youngster to use the image of "turning your body in a barrel," and I still use it today.

The right knee can straighten some but stays mainly flexed. Your weight stays centered on the balls of your feet as you swing the club back. This is critical for attaining a consistent bottom of the arc (impact position).

I maintain the slight cup in my left wrist that I started with at address to the top and into the downswing. I keep my initial grip pressure to the end of the backswing, the left hand firmer than the right. I want the left hand in control. I keep my left arm straight but not rigid.

Average golfers fall victim to TWO COMMON BACKSWING FAULTS: straightening the right knee, and sliding/swaying to the outside of the right foot. Straightening the right leg commonly causes the dreaded reverse pivot where the weight goes to the left foot during the backswing and to the right foot on the downswing—just the opposite of a correct weight shift. This causes a significant loss of club-head speed and, thus, distance.

RIGHT LEG
STRAIGHTENS   NO

Golfers trying too hard to "get behind the ball" are prone to sliding their hips rather than turning the right hip rearward. Their center of gravity shifts too far to the right and causes them to hit the ground behind the ball. Another old saying comes to mind: "Swing within your feet."

The two purposes of the backswing are to wind up the upper body to store power that will unleash in the downswing and to swing the club into position for a downswing on the right path. I want to swing back with my left arm and hand in control and my right side feeling soft and pliable. My left heel comes up to facilitate a better turn. It's old school—but it's especially helpful as I get older. It can help many of you make a fuller turn. Just be sure to return your heel to where it was.

A lot of people are afraid to turn enough. My father's and my role model for turning smoothly and fearlessly was Sam Snead. He had far and away the most fluid and powerful golf swing. When he was eighty he still was turning and swinging better than golfers half his age! At the top of his swing his left heel had come up and his shoulders had turned 90 degrees.

WEIGHT
SLIDES RIGHT NO

Sam had a lot of simple lessons to help his fellow golfers. He would tell slicers to turn their shoulders more, especially on a tight driving hole. He'd tell them to make a full turn and not "steer" the ball with just their arms. My father gave me that good advice when I was a youngster.

Sam had a pet saying: "Turn and burn! Turn and burn!" He did. Every time. Of course God gave him a lot of that ability. He was one of the most flexible men I've ever known. At eighty he could still amaze people by kicking the top of a doorjamb. With either foot.

And remember that *keeping your spine angle consistent* from address to shortly after impact is a must. A steady head is the hub of your swing.

REVIEW

→ **Turn** your lower body in the "barrel."

→ **Make** a full shoulder turn.

→ **Spine** angle stays consistent.

AT THE TOP

CHECKING YOUR position at the top of the swing is a good idea. You can have a teacher or friend be your eyes.

I want to see that my shoulders have completed their turn—90 degrees from my address position—and that my back is facing the target. Ideally when I look at the ball I see my left shoulder about an inch behind it.

My right hip has rotated back and around out of the way (the hips don't slide to the right). My left arm is straight (not stiff) and is positioned on the proper plane in "the slot" (between my head and right shoulder, not too high or too low).

My weight has stayed on the insides of my feet, my right foot flat. My right knee is slightly flexed, and my left knee has collapsed inward.

I sometimes swing a long club below parallel, but would prefer it to be parallel to the ground or just short of it. My left wrist has stayed slightly cupped at the top, which puts my left thumb under the shaft and supporting it.

SHOULD YOU PAUSE AT THE TOP?

I believe the swing should be a continuous, flowing motion, with an ever so slight pause in the club's movement as it's changing direction, when the hips are starting their forward rotation and the club is stopping its backswing and starting its downswing.

I don't like the idea of coming to a complete stop at the top. I'd prefer to see you pause slightly up there rather than make a quick, jerky change of direction from your backswing to your downswing.

I also don't like the backswing to be super slow, followed by a quick, jerky change of direction . . . no pause . . . and a rush job down from the top. The rhythm should be the same just before the end of the backswing and just into the downswing. THEN POUR IT ON! Too many people take the club back extra slooooowly, then rush down from the top as though a dog's about to run by and take the ball. Your objective should be to change direction at the same, controlled speed with no break in motion.

'I DON'T LIKE THE IDEA OF COMING TO A COMPLETE STOP AT THE TOP.'

COMMON FAULT

A poor move I see in a lot of amateurs' swings is the left shoulder pulling up at the start of the downswing. The club gets stuck behind the body, so the hands and arms don't release through the ball properly. Most shorter hitters fail to make a level shoulder turn.

At the start of the downswing, I want to keep my shoulders on the same plane they were on going back—in the same relationship to my spine angle. I almost feel my left shoulder going down and around. That's a point I've seen David Leadbetter make to his students, and he's made it to me.

FIND YOUR POSITION AT THE TOP

To be in a good position at the top of your swing, do this simple exercise.

1

- **ADDRESS** the ball as you normally would, with proper posture.

2

- **LIFT** the club and lay it on your right shoulder next to your neck, with your elbows flexed and close together.

3

- **TURN** your shoulders and hips back exactly as you would normally, with your arms swinging to the end of your backswing.

4

- Then **PUSH** your left arm out straight.

Now you're in a good position at the top of your swing. Try to mirror this position when you hit the ball.

KEEP A CONSISTENT
WRIST CUP

A KEY to swing consistency is maintaining the angle of the left wrist from address to the top and then into the downswing. My wrist is slightly cupped at address, and is the same at the end of my backswing.

I recommend this slightly cupped position. It allows me to properly hinge my wrists during the swing.

I keep that position for a foot or so into the downswing. From here, I start to release the clubhead before my left arm reaches horizontal.

A bad grip will force you to make compensations on your downswing or else hit off-line shots. A bowed position causes the club to get "laid off" and heavy-feeling at the top and the clubface to close or shut coming down. Too cupped, and the downswing is too steep and the face too open. But whatever wrist position you start with, stay with it into the downswing to consistently return the clubface to its square address position.

GOOD

TOO BOWED

TOO CUPPED

THE TRANSITION
AT THE TOP

THE TOP of the swing is a critical point. With good timing the transition from backswing to downswing is the power move. It happens fast between the backswing and downswing, but ideally you should be able to change direction at the same, controlled speed. In the transition from backswing to downswing it's the *separation* between the lower body and upper body that marks the best swings.

We'll assume that you have set up well, kept your grip pressure light, and made a full backswing turn so you feel tension in the left side of your back down to your hip. Think of turning in a barrel, not sliding your hips.

THEN AT THE TOP, THE LOWER BODY STARTS FORWARD WHEN THE UPPER BODY IS STILL GOING BACK: The left hip turns toward the target and the left heel comes down as the shoulders continue to coil. That's the separation we're talking about.

I have to say I've never had to worry about separation since my father taught me early on to finish with my belt buckle facing the target. That had the effect of speeding up my hip turn on the downswing and causing separation.

Many average golfers and short hitters start down too forcefully with the upper body. The shoulders turn toward the target too early, and the arms swing down on an outside-in path. That causes the dreaded "over the top" swing that results in slices or pulls. I tell my pro-am partners to feel lazy at the top.

Again, you should change directions at the same, controlled speed. The best modern example to me of the separation between the upper and lower body in transition is Ernie Els. The beautiful thing about his languid-looking swing is that you can see the move in action. He starts his downswing with wonderful tempo.

This key separation move creates additional torque that has to be released later, resulting in extra arm speed and power through the ball. Separation between the lower body and upper body is the key move in any sport where you need to use the hips to create arm speed—the tennis serve or baseball swing, for example.

Baseball great Ted Williams talked about it, and so did Ben Hogan. Teacher Jim Hardy, a student of Hogan's swing, said he heard that Hogan and Williams discussed the move, which Williams called his "hip cock" in his book on hitting with power.

Hogan said in his book *Five Lessons*, and I agree, that the shoulders turn the hips on the backswing, and the hips turn the shoulders on the downswing. The transition move has to be timed or else your hips tend to outrace your arms, leaving the clubface open.

The weekend golfer might not be able to master

the timing necessary to execute separation to the max, without a lot of practice at least, but almost certainly he needs to think more about the lower body leading the downswing—specifically the left hip. It's possible to move the lower body too fast on the downswing, but I rarely see that with most players.

REVIEW

→ **Left hip** reverses direction and left heel replants.

→ **Left shoulder** stays on plane.

→ **Release** club at ball with right hand.

DOWNSWING

DONE CORRECTLY, the downswing is a reflexive action, with little time to think about it. My shoulders and arms accelerate smoothly to catch up to the turning of the left hip that started first in separation. Keeping a stable head (little movement up or down or in or out) helps you stay in good balance and deliver the club squarely to the ball along the aim line.

Years ago Sam Snead and I talked about swinging around a steady head during the swing, something Sam did to perfection. I never forgot that.

The key to the proper downswing is *a consistent spine angle*. I try to turn my shoulders on the same plane or arc they turned on when I made my backswing.

I feel the timing of my downswing starts from my feet. The left heel returns to the ground and starts the counter-rotation of the hips, which in turn leads into the counter-rotation of the shoulders. That puts me in position to swing my arms fast, the payoff to a powerful downswing.

Light grip pressure here is *very* important. If your grip pressure is too tight, your hands will swing ahead of the ball and you'll hit to the right.

Many golfers wonder when the wrists and hands should uncock during the downswing. Centrifugal force should cause that to happen naturally.

A word of advice here. As I said earlier, use as strong a left-hand grip as you can without hooking the ball too much. That promotes an easier unhinging with less chance of leaving the clubface open at impact and causing a slice.

You cannot begin the unhinging too early, as Jack Nicklaus has said many times, as long as your weight has shifted onto your left foot and your hips continue to turn out of the way. Most golfers stay over on the right foot too long. They unhinge their wrists from the top and waste clubhead speed before they ever get to the ball.

Move firmly onto your left foot, turn your hips, and HIT THE BALL with your right hand! Hit it hard!

There are some very good right-sided players. Fred Couples is an excellent example of a man who fires his right side and releases the club with his right hand, his weight shifted onto his left foot. Fred's one of the most solid ball strikers I've ever seen.

Fred Couples

REVIEW

→ **Swing** around a steady head.

→ **Maintain** a consistent spine angle.

→ **Move** firmly onto your left foot.

→ **Hit** hard with your right hand.

WATSON MOMENT

A STEADY HEAD AT AUGUSTA

REMEMBER Phil Mickelson's 6-iron shot out of the trees and pine needles on the 13th hole on his way to winning the Masters in 2010? I had a similar shot—but longer—in the '86 Masters.

I hit my tee ball through the fairway on the sharp dogleg left, ending up in the pine needles looking at 210 yards to carry over the creek fronting the green on the par 5. I had to hit it through a narrow slot between two pine trees. I thought briefly about laying up, but I needed to make a run to try to catch up, so I took a chance with a 4-wood.

Your feet can slip quite easily swinging in those loose pine needles, and it was a risky play.

I had to keep my balance yet swing with force. I eliminated any thought of my feet and focused solely on keeping my head still.

It was really important to swing with a steady head.

I did, and hit the most solid high 4-wood I think I ever hit. I vividly remember that the flight of the ball was framed by the two pine trees and highlighted as it reached its zenith by a sudden flash of lightning in the darkened sky.

IMPACT

A QUESTION I get a lot is: What do you look at when you're hitting the golf ball? The answer is that I pick a dimple at the back-center of the ball to focus on, and I square the clubhead to that point. That's where I look and where I want to make contact. I narrow my focus to look at that point and that point only. And remember, contact should be made just before the club reaches the bottom of the arc.

With Byron Nelson at the 1982 Masters

I rely on a couple of keys I picked up from Sam Snead and Byron Nelson early in my career. Sam liked to work on his swing by assuming his starting position, taking the club to the top at reduced speed, then coming down and stopping at impact with his clubface square to the ball and his hips and shoulders slightly open—as in Gary Player's forward press position. Take it to the top, swing back to the ball, and stop. Try it.

Sam wanted to feel that he was in the correct position at impact relative to the position he was in at address, with the clubface square and his left arm and the shaft in straight, firm alignment. Most important was the square clubface—not open, not closed, but square. Remember, though, that the address and impact positions aren't truly mirror images. The lower body has opened some.

Byron had a wonderful tip about the impact position. He said that when he was playing his best (which may have been as good as anybody has ever played), *his hips and elbows were close to his body at impact.* If your arms separate too much from your upper body in the impact area—as often happens when we try to increase clubhead speed—you're in trouble. Byron said he wore out the right side of his slacks because his right elbow hit his right side all the time. This really helped keep his clubface square to his aim line through the impact area.

At impact, these are the action positions of the feet, knees, hips, arms, and shoulders:

1 FEET AT IMPACT
The right heel should be slightly off the ground. Most of your weight at impact should be on the left foot.

2 KNEES AT IMPACT
The right knee should be "kicked in" toward the ball. The left knee is braced and straightened from the address position. The left foot is flat on the ground, not rolled to the outside.

3 HIPS AT IMPACT
The hips are slightly opened from address position, continuing their turn (not slide) in the barrel.

4 ARMS AT IMPACT
Left arm straight. Right arm straightening but not completely straight. It fully straightens just after impact.

5 SHOULDERS AT IMPACT
Both slightly open in relation to the address position.

ADDRESS **IMPACT**

POOR IMPACT POSITIONS

I see two common poor impact positions. In one, the hands are leading too much. In the other, the right shoulder is too high: the classic "over the top" swing.

You have to make a sound swing to arrive at impact the way you should. There's no time to build in compensations on your downswing. We're trying to establish constants in our swings so we don't have to clutter our minds with too many mechanical concerns on the golf course. Always remember that on the course the swing has to be a smooth, flowing action, not a series of paint-by-the-numbers moves.

And remember: With all clubs except the driver and putter, the bottom of the arc is just ahead of the ball. Our goal is to consistently reach the bottom of the arc at the same place every time we swing the club. With the irons it's ball-divot.

'THERE'S NO TIME TO BUILD IN COMPENSATIONS ON YOUR DOWNSWING.'

REVIEW

→ **Look** at a contact point on the ball.

→ **Return** the clubface to where it started.

→ **Hips and elbows** close together at impact.

FOLLOW-THROUGH TO FINISH

YOU DON'T hit the ball with your follow-through, but practicing a proper finish and visualizing it on the course can help you be more consistent at impact.

In my time, I've seen a swing change occur on the PGA Tour. During the '90s I began to see younger players on tour swinging differently from the way I learned. They finished with the arms and club lower and more around the body. Anthony Kim is a good example today.

Jack Nicklaus had a very upright swing with a high finish for much of his career, and a lot of us tried to copy him. We were taught to finish in that "reverse C" body position that led to more than a few shots blocked out to the right and also some back problems. (Jack flattened his follow-through later in his career.)

I swung that way for many years but eventually changed to a flatter or more horizontal follow-through that gave me a straighter and lower ball flight. I became more consistent with my long game. The club can be swung more repetitively on a flatter path than on an upright path. Your upper body doesn't have to be as active.

If you think of a Ferris wheel being totally upright and a merry-go-round totally flat, your swing plane should be between those two extremes but more upright than flat, or above the 45-degree mid-point. The shorter in stature you are, the closer your plane should be to the merry-go-round; the taller you are, the closer to the Ferris wheel.

STAY CONNECTED

You need to keep your upper left arm close to your chest to swing on the proper swing plane, reach impact, and follow through to the finish consistently. We used to practice it using a handkerchief. More recently we use a folded towel. Vijay Singh works on it rigorously. Put a towel under your left armpit and hold it there throughout your swing as you hit balls, not letting it drop. That keeps your left arm closer to the turn of your body on the follow-through, producing more rotation of the forearms after impact. That will cure a slice.

CAN YOU RAISE YOUR RIGHT FOOT?

Another check is to see if you can raise your right foot off the ground when you're in your finish position. I don't want to feel any weight on my right foot at the finish. My weight has shifted onto the outside of my left foot. If you can lift your right foot, you know you've stayed in balance.

'FINISH WITH YOUR BELT BUCKLE FACING THE HOLE.'

BELT BUCKLE AT TARGET

When I was six years old and taking up the game, my father said, "All right, son, when you finish your swing, finish with your belt buckle facing the hole." Belt buckles were not flashy accessories back then—or even now with us older pros—but the thought ensures that a lot of positive things happen naturally.

At the finish of the swing your weight should be mostly on your left foot, and you should be balanced on your right toe. Practice being in this position for ten seconds, three times in a row. Then swing at a ball and try to finish in that same position you rehearsed.

RELEASE

DO YOU slice your longer shots?

If you are one of the millions who do, you aren't releasing the club through the hitting zone. As a result you never hit the ball as far as you're capable of hitting it. Most of you don't find release happening naturally, as it should be in a good swing. You need to create it—make it happen.

I release the club by rotating my forearms. Here's an easy-to-remember way to hit through the ball and release the club. *Try to touch your left forearm with your right forearm as you hit through the ball.* When you practice, rotate your forearms as fast as you can through the ball. Keep them relaxed so you can rotate them quickly. Tightness leads to slowness in the swing.

Your forearms probably won't actually touch, but the effort will lead to a better release. You may even find eventually that your slice becomes a hook and your driving distance improves dramatically.

At this stage of the swing you have no conscious control of the clubhead. But thinking about a good release before you start the swing can reduce a tendency to "block" or "steer" shots. Many average golfers rotate the club fairly naturally on the backswing but fail to rotate it back through the ball, and that's a big reason they slice.

Another good thought is to make the toe of the club pass the heel through the ball. You'll deliver an aggressive, offensive blow rather than a weak, defensive one.

REVIEW

→ **Strong grip**, closed stance to start.

→ **Rotate** your forearms through the ball.

→ **Make** the toe of the club pass the heel.

BACKSWING

HOW STAN THIRSK TEACHES RELEASE

Stan Thirsk has his students, beginners in particular, make just half swings to learn release—swinging the club back to where the left arm is straight and parallel to the ground with the club and thumbs pointing up in the air, then through to where the right arm is straight and parallel with the club and thumbs pointing up. Back and forth. Back and forth.

My pal Bob Murphy also likes to teach release this way in clinics we do together—as a quick way to stop slicing. He has students make sure the butt end of the club points at the aim line both back and through. That promotes a proper release into the follow-through.

LOWER-BODY ACTION

YOU CAN make a well-coordinated swing only if your lower body is alive and active. Otherwise the club will not go back on an arc. You will pick it up too much with your hands. We're talking now about using your hips, knees, and feet properly during the swing.

Too many of you play with what I call "cement legs." Your lower body doesn't move, so your upper body bobs up and down and your hands get too active. Inconsistency is inevitable.

Sound posture is the foundation for good lower-body action. Review the setup in chapter 2. Bend from the waist, keep your back straight and your butt out, and keep your weight on the balls and the insides of your feet. Kick your right knee in. Flex your knees and keep them flexed during the swing.

LOWER-BODY BACKSWING

At the beginning of the backswing, there is very little or no hip turn. Just the arms and shoulders are in motion. But by the time the arms and club reach waist high, the shoulder turn will cause the hips to turn in sync. (Remember to turn your hips in an imaginary barrel—don't let them slide laterally.)

Many of today's professionals restrict the hip turn on their backswings while rotating their shoulders as far as possible. That shortens their backswings, but they still achieve a tight upper-body coil.

I advise that the older you get and the less flexible you are, the more you need to turn your hips to create a fuller shoulder turn. It also puts less strain on your back.

At the end of the backswing, the left knee points at the ball or near it. The body's center of gravity hasn't moved toward the heels or toes; it remains on the balls and the insides of the feet, where it started at address. At the top of my swing I want to see no daylight under the ball of my right foot—no "spikes" showing—or I've gone too far.

Remember to kick your right knee in at address.

LOWER-BODY DOWNSWING

The downswing starts with the counter-rotation of the left hip. That stops the backswing rotation of the shoulders.

I like to see golfers get a little aggressive with their knees when starting the downswing. If you've set up with your knees straight, you're beaten before you start. Remember, your shoulders turn your hips on the backswing, but your hips turn your shoulders on the downswing.

Point your left knee at the ball on your backswing— at impact your right knee should be pointed at the ball. Think of a left knee/right knee swing motion.

At impact the hips have quickly rotated to a slightly open position from their address position. The left foot has planted firmly on the ground with most of your weight shifted onto that foot.

I repeat for emphasis. *The center of gravity remains on the balls and insides of your feet, which keeps your head steady.*

When my footwork goes off, I often concentrate on my lower body to get my timing back. I feel with my feet in a real sense. It's possible to use your lower body too much, but weekend golfers hardly ever do.

1 ADDRESS

2 BACKSWING

3 IMPACT

Weight stays on balls of feet.

RHYTHM

WE'VE COVERED the mechanical elements of the swing. What's the glue we need to hold these elements together? It's rhythm or tempo, of course. Consistent rhythm/tempo produces consistent timing of the hit.

If your mechanics are correct (your grip, address position, takeaway, transition), then your particular consistent rhythm completes the package. Consistent rhythm equals a consistently square clubface at impact. Inconsistent rhythm equals mis-hits and misdirected shots. Consistent rhythm lets your mechanics work consistently.

Different people have different swing tempos. Myself, I have a fast rhythm. So does Nick Price. Then look at Ernie Els and Fred Couples. They have slow rhythms. You should swing with your natural rhythm, one that reflects your temperament. The key to a consistent swing is learning to repeat the same rhythm, be it slow or fast, with each swing.

FAST RHYTHM: WATSON

FAST RHYTHM: PRICE

SLOW RHYTHM: COUPLES

SLOW RHYTHM: ELS

'I VISUALIZED SAM'S SWING WHEN MY TIMING WENT OFF. HIS KEY WAS LIGHT GRIP PRESSURE AND RELAXED ARMS, PARTICULARLY HIS RIGHT ARM.'

Probably the best rhythm I ever saw was Sam Snead's. I looked forward to the Masters every year because I could watch him practice. He called his rhythm "oily"—a good word for it. I visualized Sam's swing when my timing went off. His key was light grip pressure and relaxed arms, particularly his right arm. He took a long, relaxed waggle immediately before starting the club back, turned his head slightly to the right, then eased into that flowing backswing.

Sam's transition from backswing to downswing was NEVER rushed. His follow-through to the finish was ALWAYS powerful and balanced, all because of his natural "oily" rhythm. Everything in his swing was graceful and unforced.

I'd recommend that anyone with a DVD player get a video with Sam's swing. His tempo will be contagious. It certainly was for me and my fellow pros, who would drop everything to watch him practice. Under pressure I've often called up a mental picture and feel of Sam's tempo as my last thought before I make my swing. It works.

A fan, an average golfer, sent me a letter a number of years ago about how he achieves consistent rhythm in his golf swing. He says the word "edelweiss" to himself, not fast but slowly. This creates a proper tempo for his golf swing. He said he timed his swing to the three syllables: e-del-weiss. The first syllable took him about halfway to the top, the second to the top, and the third down through impact. Back and forth, e-del-weiss, over and over.

His advice sounded kind of goofy, but I tried it and it worked! One of my favorite movies, *The Sound of Music,* is even more special to me now.

Some people's "edelweiss" may be faster or slower than my "edelweiss," but I like the term

because it allows any of us to swing in rhythm consistently, no matter how fast or slow our tempo is. Even when you putt. My swing is fast, but not so fast that the movements don't happen in the correct sequence, IF I maintain a consistent tempo. This is where "edelweiss" comes into play. I think the most important thing for you is to work with one simple, positive thought about good rhythm before you ever address the ball.

During tournament play or your weekend games, acknowledge that pressure is always present. It pushes you to go faster than your normal rhythm in both your thinking and your play, so that you need to make a concerted effort to slow down. Byron Nelson said that when he got under pressure, he always walked and thought too fast. He told me, "Tom, do two things. Walk a little slower, and breathe a little deeper. This will help slow down not only your ac-

tions, but your thinking as well. Pressure will not go away, but physically dealing with it in this way will help you get along with it better." Great advice from a man who understood what pressure was.

You will actually see me yawning under pressure. No, I am NOT falling asleep. I'm filling my lungs with as much air as I can put in them.

REVIEW
→ **Know** your
  natural rhythm.

→ **Watch** video of
  Sam Snead's swing.

→ **Try** "e-del-weiss."

→ **Walk** slower, breathe
  deeper. (Yawn.)

PAVIN'S PRACTICE SWING

DISCOVERING
MY SECRET

GRATEFULLY I discovered the secret to my golf swing on tour at Harbour Town in 1994 after a particularly poor practice round during the Heritage Golf Classic. I was hitting the ball consistently to the right with toe-deep divots, a tendency that had plagued me throughout my career.

Back in those days I was still swinging the club into a "reverse C" position at impact. I drove my legs toward the target vigorously from the top of the swing with both knees flexed, or soft, at impact, causing my left shoulder to be too high and my right shoulder too low at impact. This move led to the clubhead staying behind me too much on the downswing—and producing a late hit with an open face. My natural reaction was to release the club earlier in the downswing—causing inconsistent timing at impact.

I was sick and tired of hitting the ball out to right field. I wanted to make the club go left through impact. But how? Somewhat in desperation I thought about Corey Pavin and his unusual practice swing, where he swings the club with an exaggerated inside path on the backswing, then outside on the downswing loop. "Coming over the top" with a high right shoulder is what this motion is commonly called, a much misused excuse for a variety of missed shots.

1980

2009

When many years later I asked Corey why he made his practice swing this way, he said he makes an exaggerated move to encourage himself to swing the club on the same path on both his backswing and downswing. At impact he was trying to keep his right shoulder higher, preventing the "reverse C" position at impact. He wanted to feel as if he was "coming over the top" with his right shoulder to make the proper swing. He didn't care what his practice swing looked like if it helped him develop a new feel to

correct a bad habit. His real swing ended up being what he wanted, with his shoulders right on plane rather than too tilted on the downswing.

Venting my frustration, I took a 3-iron and made a swing the way I envisioned his practice swing. My right shoulder felt as though it went out and around on the downswing. I hit three perfect shots in a row with divots nice and even, not toe deep. The club swung left through impact without my hands having to release too early to try to square up the club. I'd never felt so much freedom in my swing. I hit more and more balls with consistently good results.

My shoulder plane went from being severely tilted to more level. Corey's practice swing got me on the same plane back and through. My spine angle started and stayed consistent. I all but eliminated shots out to the right, and I took a lot of stress off my back.

The modern touring professional's swing has evolved to this level shoulder turn and more rotation around the body. We from the old school have learned that it makes for a more consistent swing. May my "secret" work for you.

'I WAS SICK AND TIRED OF HITTING THE BALL OUT TO RIGHT FIELD. I WANTED TO MAKE THE CLUB GO LEFT THROUGH IMPACT.'

Watch Tom Watson giving a demonstration of one of the lessons featured within this chapter. Go to http://gettag.mobi for your free mobile app, then point your smartphone's camera at the Microsoft Tag and enjoy the video.

LEARNING THE SHOULDER PLANE

Since I found the way to keep my shoulders more level on the downswing, I teach shoulder-plane rotation this way. I ask you to stand up straight and put a club across your shoulders at the back of your neck, parallel to the ground. (I sometimes use a rod to dramatize it, or a broom is lightweight and works.) Your head is up.

The club is perpendicular to the axis of your spine. Rotate your shoulders back so the club stays parallel to the ground. Then mirror that rotation on your forward swing, keeping the club parallel to the ground.

When you bend from the waist to simulate a real swing from your normal address position, *you must maintain a consistent spine angle.* You still turn your shoulders back and forth in the same plane, *perpendicular to your now-bent-over spine angle,* as you did when you were standing straight up. But now the club does not stay parallel to the ground, because you have bent over.

My right shoulder is always slightly lower than my left shoulder because my right hand is lower on the grip. But my right shoulder had been *too low at impact, my left shoulder too high* before I copied Corey's practice swing with its high right shoulder position at impact.

The proper shoulder rotation follows only from a spine angle that is stationary or close to stationary from address through impact. It keeps your head from bobbing up and down. Turn your shoulders around the base of your neck with a steady head.

'THE PROPER SHOULDER ROTATION
FOLLOWS ONLY FROM A SPINE ANGLE THAT
IS STATIONARY OR CLOSE TO STATIONARY
FROM ADDRESS THROUGH IMPACT.'

'I TRY TO MAKE EVERY SHOT DROP EITHER LEFT OR RIGHT. A STRAIGHT SHOT'S AN ACCIDENT.'

→ BE A
SHOTMAKER

121

4

BE A SHOTMAKER

SO FAR WE'VE FOCUSED ON THE KEY FUNDAMENTALS of the golf swing as I understand them: the factors you must be able to repeat consistently. Before moving on, make sure you understand—and can apply—those basics. Review the earlier chapters periodically. Realistically, mastering the basics requires a reasonable amount of practice, the same as anything else you want to improve. Positive practice, where you're working on the right things and not just beating balls or seeing how far you can hit your driver. The next step is learning to control and maneuver the ball. Expanding your shotmaking skill is extremely useful—it's essential to good strategy and course management—and it's great fun!

BALL CONTROL

YOU DON'T have to be a low-handicapper to hit a low hook or a high slice on call. The benefits are several. You can learn about spin and how the ball reacts to it; you can change your basic shot pattern once and for all—from a weak slice to a strong hook, for example; you can get out of trouble by avoiding an obstacle like a tree; you can play a dogleg hole the way the architect designed it; you can get the ball closer to a tucked hole location.

Different teachers and players use different methods to maneuver the ball. Generally they involve adjustments in grip, aim, and alignment that are not difficult to master. Today's balls are harder to spin and curve, but you still can shape shots—and need to. I try to make every shot drop either left or right. A straight shot's an accident.

Let's learn how to apply the fundamentals to become a more complete player.

WHAT ARE YOUR OPTIONS?

CLOSED STANCE

HOW TO HOOK (AND FIX YOUR SLICE)

AT LEAST 90 percent of you slice the ball, losing accuracy and distance. If you can learn to hook, you can banish that hated slice forever. And get around the course with better strategy. There are different ways you can move the ball from right to left.

MY DAD'S WAY

My dad, a good golfer, was nicknamed "Hook." He could hit all the shots, but his natural curve was a hook. When I was learning to play at age six, Dad taught me to hook his way. He said, "Son, aim to the right of the target, hold the club more loosely, pull your right foot back, and when you go through the impact area, rotate your hands a little faster. It will hook."

JACK'S WAY

I saw Jack Nicklaus do a clinic and show a good way of teaching a hook. He said to hold the club out in front of you, hood or close the clubface, then regrip the club with the face hooded.

With the club looking to the left, you have to aim to the right of your target so the ball won't start too far left. Swing along your new aim line with the hooded face—and the result is a hook. Experiment to find the best combination of hooded face and aim to the right.

Hold loosely . . .   **. . . then regrip.**

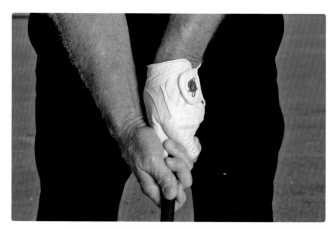

A CAUTION: Strengthen your grip. When you adjust your grip, keep the clubface aimed where it was. Don't turn it as you turn your hands.

EASIEST WAY FOR YOU

A third way to hook may be the easiest for most of you. Simply strengthen your grip. Place your left hand on the club first, rotating it so you see THREE knuckles instead of the two you see in a neutral grip. Your left thumb should run farther over toward the right side of the shaft. When you put your right hand on, make sure it too is turned more under the shaft. It's important to turn your right hand as much as your left. Your palms should remain facing.

THE OBJECT of all three of these methods is to arrive at impact with a closed clubface.

In some cases you need to hit an EXTREME HOOK. This is a lot of fun. You use it to get around trees, for example. To do it, you combine all three methods.

Turn the clubhead so the face is closed (aimed left), then take a stronger grip with both hands. Rotate your hands faster through the impact area. You'll hit a smother-hook. Make sure you aim properly, well right of the target. Go to the practice range and find the right aim line.

Watch Tom Watson giving a demonstration of one of the lessons featured within this chapter. Go to http://gettag.mobi for your free mobile app, then point your smartphone's camera at the Microsoft Tag and enjoy the video.

HOOK >

> TARGET
LINE

< AIM LINE

OPEN STANCE

HOW TO SLICE (AND FIX YOUR HOOK)

MOST OF you know slicing all too well and probably don't want to dwell on it. The club delivers a glancing blow, causing the ball to go higher and shorter with more backspin. But to be able to hit a slice on call is a necessary component of a complete player's game. It can get you around trouble. It also can help you tame a hook if that's your problem. Hitting a slice, you do pretty much the opposite of everything I said about the hook.

MY DAD'S WAY

My dad also taught me to slice. He said, "Son, open up your stance, open up the clubface at address, hold on tighter with the last three fingers of the left hand, take the club back on the outside, and then cut across the ball and make the club finish low and left." That's what I did, and it made the ball slice.

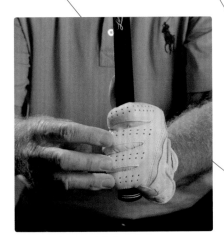

Grip tighter with last three fingers of left hand.

JACK'S WAY

A second method is the Nicklaus method. You first release or loosen your grip, open the clubface from its square position, then regrip the club with your normal grip. Aim the face, now open, at the target, but align your stance and body left of your target. Then make your normal swing. Swinging with an open clubface will cause the ball to slice, starting left of your target and curving left to right toward it.

'AIM THE FACE, NOW OPEN, AT THE TARGET, BUT ALIGN YOUR STANCE AND BODY LEFT OF YOUR TARGET.'

CHANGE YOUR GRIP

The third method is simply to change your grip. From a "neutral" grip, seeing two knuckles of the left hand with the "V's" of both hands pointing to the right shoulder, deliberately "weaken" your grip. From their normal position, move both hands to the left, running your left thumb straight down the top of the club and turning your right hand to the left. The "V's" point more toward your chin or just left of it. With this method you aim both the clubface and your body left of the target and make your normal swing. An open clubface at impact causes a slice.

Lastly, if you want to hit an *extreme slice*, combine cutting across the ball, weakening the grip, and the Nicklaus method: You will move the ball from left to right—guaranteed!

SLICE

AIM
LINE

TARGET
LINE

HITTING HIGH SHOTS

THE MAIN thing is to hit the ball slightly before the *very bottom* of the arc. Refer back to chapter 1 if you need to. The bottom of the arc is crucial to every shot we hit—especially irons off the ground.

I set up raising my left shoulder and lowering my right shoulder. I play the ball an inch farther forward than usual in my stance, to add loft to the clubface (make sure you keep the clubface square). I also stand an inch or so closer to the ball, to avoid hitting it off the toe of the club.

Kick your right knee in toward your left knee as a brace. Swing thoughts: make a wide backswing, keep your head behind the ball as you hit it, and finish with your hands high. A high finish means a high shot.

To add height, weaken your grip by setting your left thumb straight down the shaft or even a bit left of that. This adjustment guarantees a more lofted clubface, and the ball will fade or slice.

I select one more club than usual to hit the ball higher—a 6-iron rather than a 7-iron, for instance—because I'll lose distance. More than one club into the wind. Whatever the club, you need to swing hard to generate enough speed to spin the ball higher. You have to hit the ball controlled-hard.

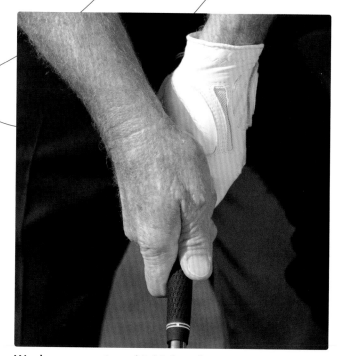

Weaken your grip to hit higher shots.

HITTING LOW SHOTS

A GREAT benefit of learning my "secret" was improving my ability to hit low shots. Simply said, leveling my shoulders coming through the ball produces a lower ball flight. I had always been a high-ball hitter, but now I'm able to control the ball better in the wind, or on a trouble shot under tree limbs, or playing a bounce-and-run approach onto a green.

With level shoulders at address, I could move the ball back in my stance and feel more comfortable at impact. Many times I move the ball back to the center of my stance—sometimes farther back.

Now I can set up with my right shoulder higher. My eyes are looking back at the ball at impact. As I swing, I think of one of two things: Keep my right shoulder higher or my left shoulder lower at impact. I keep my left shoulder low, and the ball is going to go low.

For this shot, like the high shot, stand an inch closer to the ball, or you'll hit the ball off the toe.

Figure on the shot rolling out more and going farther. You might want to choose less club. I want to finish low for a low shot. And again we want ball-divot contact.

I have to credit Lee Trevino, probably the best low-ball hitter ever, for helping me learn to hit the ball lower.

Lee Trevino

WATSON MOMENT

*K*EEPING IT DOWN IN THE OPEN

AN EXAMPLE of executing a low shot was a 5-iron approach I hit to the 10th green in the British Open at Turnberry in 2009. It's a long par 4 with water on the left, and it was playing into the wind.

I hit it to about 30 feet with a lower trajectory than normal so it would roll after it landed short of the green, and made a solid par to keep my round going. I did all the things I talk about here, including moving the ball back and finishing low.

THE HIGH HOOK

THIS ONE'S tougher than the low hook. You must really release the club through the ball, and finish high.

First put the ball forward in your stance. Aim the clubface at your target, but align your body to the right. Swing the club away low to the ground, and make sure to keep your head behind the ball at impact.

Feel that you are releasing the clubhead out and up. Finish with your hands high.

THE LOW HOOK

THIS IS a relatively easy shot. Just smother-hook it. Close the club face—turn it 30 degrees to the left. Strengthen your grip to see three knuckles on your left hand. Position the ball back of center in your stance. Aim and swing well right of your target line.

Strongly release the clubhead through impact, making the toe of the head pass the heel.

WARNING: Be sure to pick a club with enough loft to get the ball up in the air.

THE HIGH
SLICE

HERE'S A shot most of you would like to be rid of, but there's a time and place for it. Just be sure to keep the clubface open through the ball.

Position the ball forward in your stance and an inch or so closer to you. Weaken your grip. Keep your left grip tighter. Use the same aim and alignment as you would for the low slice. Swing the club outside and up (compared to your normal swing). Then swing down, keep your head back, and finish with your hands high.

THE LOW
SLICE

THIS IS another true tester, though many of you have a head start with slicing. The hard part is keeping the ball down. I'll move it back in my stance to keep from hitting it too high. Gripping down on the club also helps. Weaken your grip from neutral.

Aim the clubface at the target, align your body left, and swing along your stance line. I block the shot hard with my hands, keeping my wrists from releasing on the downswing and making sure the club does not—repeat NOT—pass the heel through the ball. Does not release.

Finish your swing very low and left, pulling your arms across your body and shutting off your follow-through.

THE FULL SAND SWING

MANY GOLFERS find this shot scary because they tend to hit behind the ball. It comes out like a "puff" ball and goes nowhere. It's not like a regular sand shot. Your key thought is to *contact the ball before the clubhead hits the sand.*

First, work your feet into the sand so they don't move during your swing. Grip up about an inch on the club, as you would on any sand shot to offset your feet being dug in. Address the ball as you normally would, without touching the sand—but just before you take the club back, kick your right knee in and lean slightly toward the target so you start and keep your weight on your left side for the entire swing. That ensures that the clubhead comes into the ball on a downward path. Again, hit the back of the ball first, before you take any sand.

The ball will probably come out lower, so factor that into your club selection. Above all, make sure you take a club that will get the ball over the front lip of the bunker and advance it. The new hybrid clubs are very good in the sand because their broader soles won't dig into the sand and cause fat shots that come up well short of your target.

KICK RIGHT
KNEE IN
→

MORE
WEIGHT ON
LEFT FOOT

MORE
WEIGHT ON
LEFT FOOT

SWINGING IN THE WIND

KNOWING HOW wind will affect the ball determines your club selection and aim. Modern metal-headed drivers perform better in the wind, launching the ball higher downwind and spinning the ball less into the wind.

But you still need to understand that a HEADWIND causes the ball to rise faster and roll less. *Golf Digest* has reported that you lose about 17 yards of carry and roll for every 10 miles per hour of headwind. That was for a typical PGA Tour pro's launch condition with a driver. (A downwind shot is affected less, as we will see.)

In my early years playing the game, I learned the hard way when my shots into the wind ended up both short and off line. I'd balloon shot after shot into a strong headwind. My teacher Stan Thirsk would constantly tell me to "Swing with ease against a breeze." I finally got it.

Swinging easier, the ball flies lower and straighter because it has less backspin and sidespin. The caveat is that you have to use more club—a stronger club, with less loft. Most of the time average golfers

RIGHT TO LEFT: I'm factoring a stiff breeze into this pitch shot, playing it right of the flag so the wind will blow it on target.

don't take nearly enough club or swing easier into a strong wind. Often I will advise them to take three more clubs than they think and just swing easier. Seeing the smiles that light up their faces when they succeed is rewarding.

We talked earlier about how you can hit the ball lower: move the ball back in your stance, raise your right shoulder at address, widen your stance, and shorten your follow-through. It's been called a "punch shot," or in modern times a "stinger," a term made popular by Tiger Woods, who often plays it with a long iron off the tee to keep the ball in play.

A DOWNWIND SHOT, on the other hand, gains only about 10 yards for every 10 miles per hour of tailwind, according to the same *Golf Digest* study. Hitting the ball higher is the key with the wind helping; the higher the flight, the farther it flies.

If your driver flight is naturally low, hitting a 3-wood off the tee will help you drive it farther downwind. Jack Nicklaus once told me he used a 3-wood rather than a driver off the tee downwind on the links courses during the British Open, and hit it farther. Elevation is the answer.

'HITTING THE BALL HIGHER IS THE KEY WITH THE WIND HELPING.'

SOLVING CROSSWINDS

In crosswinds be mindful of your ball's natural curve. If you slice the ball with a left-to-right wind, it will travel farther than the normal distance you hit that club. If you hook the ball with that same left-to-right wind, the ball will travel shorter than normal.

With a right-to-left crosswind, the reverse is true for your natural slice or hook. Be aware of those influences.

Especially playing the British Open, I always remind myself to think of the break in a green when dealing with the strong crosswind on full shots. The wind will act as "slope" and make the ball curve, the way it would curve on a breaking putt.

Give a crosswind its due! Play for more curve than you might think. Most amateurs I play with don't adjust their aim nearly enough. Move your aiming point or goalposts. Many, many times I've aimed well left or right of the fairway or green in a strong crosswind. The ball will curve 30 or 40 yards or more.

Some useful advice: On windy days go to the practice tee with a laser range finder and determine the distance you hit a particular club with a particular wind. That will teach you to choose the proper club in windy conditions.

The 11th hole at Birkdale, with a right-to-left wind.

WATSON MOMENT

GOALPOSTS AT BIRKDALE

PLAYING in the wind is common at The Open and is much discussed by golfers enjoying the links courses of the UK. Choosing an aim line in a crosswind is difficult, but if I had to say one thing about how to do it, it would be to allow more for the wind than what you think, especially when it's howling.

I was playing the elevated tee at the par-4 11th hole in the first round at Royal Birkdale in the 2008 Open Championship, and it taught me a good lesson. With at least a 35-mph crosswind from right to left, I applied my goalposts aiming method. I envisioned the center of my goalposts to be the right edge of the fairway.

When I hit my tee ball, I knew immediately my aim was wrong. The ball started just left of my imagined center and hooked with the wind some 20 yards into the rough on the left. Bogey.

Playing the tee shot at the 11th the next day with the very same crosswind, I moved the center of my goalposts about 40 yards right of the right edge of the fairway! This time the ball found the fairway. I had learned the hard way the previous day. That tee shot has always stuck in my mind because of how far off the fairway I had to aim to get the ball in the short grass.

→ SWING YOUNGER

'IT'S NEVER TOO LATE FOR OLDER GOLFERS TO LEARN NEW TRICKS.'

149

5 SWING YOUNGER

IF YOUR HEALTH HOLDS UP, you usually can play deep into your senior years. It's never too late for older golfers to learn new tricks. That's what this next section is about. When I think of aging gracefully in our sport, I think of Sandy Tatum, a good friend since my college days at Stanford. I met Sandy when our team played the alumni—they cleaned our clock. Sandy was NCAA champion there earlier, and went on to become a Rhodes Scholar and practice law successfully in San Francisco. He was president of the U.S. Golf Association and has long been an articulate spokesman for everything good about our sport. He was for many years my partner in the Crosby Pro-Am. He's into his nineties now and still playing well enough to enjoy it. He keeps flexible by stretching every day. His swing key is still making a big shoulder turn. Swing the arms and shoulders as far back around and up as possible without losing the firmness of the left arm. That's a key thought when you're facing the later years of your golfing life. A few more thoughts follow.

HOW TO DRIVE IT FARTHER

EVERY GOLFER of any age I've ever known—myself included—would like to hit the ball farther. The shot you talk about after a round is probably the time you out-drove your main competitor. When I need extra distance, this is what I do, especially nowadays in my sixties. I think it can work for you.

I *adjust my stance* to turn my left toe out more, so it's about 30 degrees open. That helps me clear my left side faster on my downswing, creating faster arm speed.

I maintain *very light grip pressure*. When you're swinging hard, you want to be able to return the clubface squarely to the ball. If you grip too tightly, you'll probably rush your downswing and get the handle too far ahead of the clubhead, causing a pushed shot. Or you'll overwork your shoulders and come over the top. Grip pressure is very important. Keep it light.

I want to take the club back on *as wide an arc as possible*, all the way to the top. That will create more centrifugal force and clubhead speed through the ball.

I want to *make a complete shoulder turn*—one that is slower and longer. I want to move my shoulders back and around as far as I can without shifting my center of gravity.

Remember when we discussed the separation at the top of the swing? I want to start down at the same speed I finished my backswing, leading with my lower body, then swing my arms fast and hit the heck out of it with my right hand! We may not be as quick and flexible as we were in our younger days, but we don't have to be overly conservative.

Most golfers are too conservative swinging the club. You have to swing past the ball.

Forget about all the mechanics and positions that might be cluttering your mind—think about swinging freely. Release the clubhead. Trapshooting is one of my favorite hobbies. I started nailing a lot more clay pigeons when my good friend Leo George told me to "Get reckless!" You have to swing the gun aggressively past the clay target; you have to lead it. The golf swing requires the same kind of uninhibited action.

'I WANT TO MAKE A COMPLETE SHOULDER TURN—ONE THAT IS SLOWER AND LONGER.'

WARNING: Golfers get into trouble trying to delay the unhinging of the wrists if their hip turn slows down or stops on the downswing. That causes a severe power shortage at impact. At impact the left hip should be slightly open from your address position.

BE A LITTLE RECKLESS

Obviously you don't want to swing out of control and lose your balance, but you can't be tentative. Learn how quickly you can move. Find the rhythm that will keep your body parts in sync and generate extra power.

Average golfers often tell each other to swing easier. It can be good advice. But you'll never be as good as you can be if you don't learn to hit the ball hard. You might think pros like Ernie Els and Fred Couples are swinging easy, but look at their tremendous clubhead speed: more than 120 miles an hour. The speed in their swings builds gradually and maxes out where it counts: through the ball and no sooner.

As Al Geiberger once said, you get one fast moment per swing. It shouldn't come before impact. The great Ben Hogan had the ability to delay the unhinging of his wrists until well into his downswing, then really turn the club loose. That takes strength and timing and a lot of practice, but if you're looking for more distance, it's worth experimenting to find out how long you can keep your wrists cocked and still make square contact.

'YOU'LL NEVER BE AS GOOD AS YOU CAN BE **IF YOU DON'T LEARN TO** HIT THE BALL HARD.'

CHECK YOUR EQUIPMENT

Have you checked your equipment to see if it's encouraging your maximum distance? In this era, power is important at all levels of play, and technological improvements in equipment come frequently for all age groups. It's like the automobile industry: some annual changes are aesthetic (which carries its own appeal), but some are substantive and advance performance.

The best way to get the right equipment is to be tested on a launch monitor with professional oversight. Many courses and golf shops make them accessible nowadays. They measure such things as launch angle and spin rate and how changing variables such as the shaft flex and clubhead loft can have a big effect on total distance. (Sometimes adding loft to a driver is the best way to improve distance.)

Longer, bigger-headed drivers with lighter shafts are popular, with good reason. The clubheads provide greater stability on off-center hits. But you still need to make solid contact consistently, so see if you can control the oversized drivers, and make sure you buy one that fits your physical ability and swing.

Years ago I felt that the average golfer would play better teeing off with a fairway wood, but no longer. The drivers with 460 cc heads—fitted properly for length, weight, flex, and loft—can be more forgiving. Again, a quality launch monitor should be able to test you for differences in those clubs and how they influence your distance and shot-dispersion patterns.

A good monitor also can provide insight into the best club-ball combination for you. Balls are becoming more specialized every year, and can be matched to your game.

LET KIDS SWING HARD

Realize that kids like our kids and grandkids want to hit the ball as far as they can. We should encourage them and teach them to swing hard. Just make sure they stay in balance.

I don't care so much if they fall forward swinging through the ball, but falling backward is bad. Teach kids to hit the ball hard. That's how I was taught as a youngster, and the advice helped me. I'm confident it can help other kids as well.

STRETCH THE
HAMSTRINGS

HERE'S A quick warm-up or practice exercise to keep your swing long.

First, bend over with flexed knees and your lower back rounded and try to touch your toes. Slowly straighten your knees a little bit to stretch the hamstrings.

Second, put a club over your shoulders, assume a correct address posture, and turn back and forth a few times. Then turn back as far as you comfortably can, hold it, release it through. That relaxes the back.

MOVE THE BALL BACK IN YOUR STANCE

MOST OF us need to adjust our ball position as we get older. I've heard that even Ben Hogan moved the ball back with advancing age. And/or if you have trouble shifting your weight through the shot, you probably should try moving the ball back somewhat. Playing from bad lies, you also need to move it back.

I used to play the ball more forward in my stance, but the bottom of my swing arc moved back because my hips turn more slowly now. Moving the ball back helps me make consistent contact and control my distance—especially with irons off the ground when I want to hit the ball first, then take a divot.

STRENGTHEN
YOUR GRIP

I'VE TALKED about the virtues of a stronger grip for most golfers who slice the ball. It can help older golfers worried about losing distance off the tee, because it encourages an easier release of the club through impact.

Try turning your hands more clockwise on the grip, so you see three knuckles on the back of your left hand. Move your right hand more under the club too.

Lighten your grip pressure in the left hand so your right hand takes over at the bottom of your swing and makes the ball hook. But be sure you grip firmly enough with your left hand to control the club.

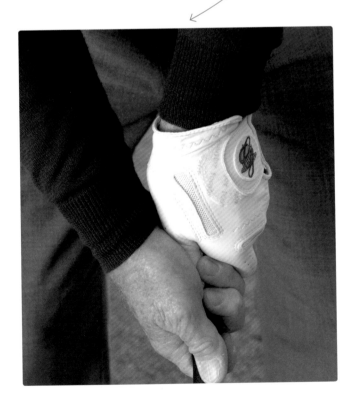

PULL YOUR RIGHT FOOT BACK

AS WE get older, pulling the right foot back makes it easier to turn the hips. Put your left foot forward slightly to close your stance.

Now you're set up to hit the ball from right to left rather than slice it weakly to the right. Your distance should improve.

TURN YOUR HIPS

WHEN THE guys on the regular tour start the club back, their hips hardly move because they want to create a lot of torque for power. But you lose that kind of flexibility as you get older, so start with your hips as well as your stance slightly closed at address. This will help you make a fuller shoulder turn on the backswing. Then start the downswing with your left hip rotating slightly before your shoulders. Think of that old "turn in a barrel" image.

Watch Tom Watson giving a demonstration of one of the lessons featured within this chapter. Go to http://gettag .mobi for your free mobile app, then point your smart-phone's camera at the Microsoft Tag and enjoy the video.

LET YOUR LEFT HEEL COME UP

LETTING YOUR left heel come up off the ground on the backswing can help you make a full turn as you get older or if you're stiff in the trunk area. I've never been as flexible as some players and I have a long backswing, so I've always let my heel come up.

You have to make sure your body stays in control, and you must re-plant the left heel where it was as you start down. But it's a good way to complete your backswing consistently. The longer the club, the more the heel lifts.

Some young players can swing flat-footed and coil fully. That's fine if you can do it. If not, try letting your left heel come up.

YES

TEE IT HIGH

YOU WOULD think that swinging the modern big-headed drivers is the same as swinging the old smaller-headed models. But you have to tee the ball higher to improve your chances of making contact on the sweet spot because the sweet spot is higher on the clubface.

I'll lower the tee a little to hit low drives or raise it a little to really fly it out there. But my normal tee position is with the *equator of the ball even with the top of my driver.*

When I converted to the big new drivers, I often hit the ball off the heel of the clubhead. I must've been hitting it in the same place relative to the shaft and not allowing for the larger size. I had to hit the ball farther out on the face to get the best results.

WATSON MOMENT

Hitting it Harder in Arizona

THE drivable par 4 is popular with many modern course architects and course setup people. It adds an exciting dimension, especially in major championships like the U.S. Open, where the use of a shorter tee means the possibility of an eagle quickly changing the leaderboard. Or a gamble that turns out badly quickly working the other way.

A personal case in point: When I played the short and challenging par-4 17th at the TPC Scottsdale in the Phoenix Open, I occasionally tried to drive the green going downwind. The hole is dotted with cross bunkers, and the green is guarded by water on the left. Into the wind I had no chance to reach the green.

The last time I played the 17th I drove the green and made an easy birdie. But over the years I also made some bogeys or worse that were hard on my ego.

When we golfers see an opportunity to go for it on a short par 4, we usually are forced to swing about as hard as we can to create more clubhead speed—and hope for a solid hit. I rarely do this, but occasionally circumstances lead me to. Waiting to hit that last tee shot on 17 in Scottsdale, I remember drawing on three swing thoughts as I waited for the green to clear. Try them if you want to hit a bigger drive.

—I told myself to make a smooth, wide takeaway, low and slow.

—To turn my shoulders a bit more on the backswing, giving my arms more time to build extra speed on the downswing.

—And last and most important, to let the club enjoy a moment of "grace" at the top of the swing, then pour it on. Don't be jerky in transition.

→ **DRILLS FOR A BETTER SWING**

'AIMLESS PRACTICE—JUST HITTING BALLS FOR THE SAKE OF HITTING BALLS—USUALLY JUST MAKES FOR INGRAINING POOR HABITS.'

6 DRILLS
FOR A BETTER SWING

IF YOU KNOW AND PRACTICE THE FUNDAMENTALS, you eventually can play by feel. But you must practice the correct things. Practice doesn't make perfect. Purposeful, smart practice makes perfect. Aimless practice— just hitting balls for the sake of hitting balls—usually just makes for ingraining poor habits. Be specific when you practice. Pick a goal or key to your swing or setup. Practice it until you reach an improved level of success. When you play on the course, don't overdo the swing thoughts. Try to think of just one at a time. Practice your drills with regularity and you'll succeed. I have found over the years that it's simple drills that make practice interesting and fun. I'll offer a few of my favorites in this section.

PRACTICE LIKE A PRO

I know you probably devote much less time to practice than we professionals do, but I encourage you to spend at least 30 minutes a couple of days a week working on your fundamentals. An hour three days a week would be better.

To me, practice is enjoyable and rewarding. I get great satisfaction out of hitting good shots. I always practice with a purpose. I work on my posture, for example, or my ball position. (It surprises people to learn that a tournament range is busy with pros working on the basics.)

One secret of Jack Nicklaus's greatness is that he never hit a careless practice shot. Never.

PUT CLUBS DOWN

A GOOD way to check your alignment is to put clubs on the ground at the range. Tour pros do it all the time, sometimes with colored rods rather than clubs.

Put a club down outside the ball representing your starting aim line, and place another club down along your toe line, parallel to the first club. Then hold a third club parallel to those two lines across your thighs and, after that, across your chest to square up your body. Memorize this position.

And let's not forget your eyes. It's possible to align your body accurately but set your eyes off line. Look at your target by *swiveling* your head, *not lifting it*. Your eye line should be parallel to your aim and body lines.

If the eyes are cocked to the right of your target, your shots are prone to go there, and vice versa. I've had quite a bit of success changing pro-am partners' eye positions just half an inch to get them hitting the ball more where they wanted it to go. You can achieve this yourself by holding that third club on your eye line and making sure it's parallel to your body lines.

Remember: Make all your aim lines parallel to one another. This is a key to the pros' consistency.

THE SHADOW KNOWS

I FIND it instructive to practice with the sun behind me when I can. That casts a shadow over the ball, and I can "see" my swing better. I like it best when the shadow is a little bit left of my ball.

From this position, I can see if I'm turning correctly and check where my club is at the top of my backswing.

PUT
YOUR
FEET
TOGETHER

THIS SIMPLE exercise—swinging with your feet together—has probably promoted more good swing results than any other drill. Everybody from Bobby Jones to Jack Nicklaus and today's top players has practiced it. The feet-together drill encourages you to swing your arms and turn your body "in the barrel."

On the range, start with a short iron and the ball teed. Swing slowly at first, gradually increasing your pace as you gain a good sense of balance. (You'll be surprised how far you can hit the ball this way with a little work!)

Gradually widen your stance and work up to longer clubs. But remember how it felt with your feet together. If you lose that feeling, go back to practicing with your feet together until you regain your balance and timing.

REGAIN YOUR TIMING

HERE'S SOMETHING you can try when the heat's on and you've really lost the feel of the clubhead— when you've lost your timing. Grip the club at the opposite end—the clubhead end instead of the handle end—and make a few practice swings.

Slow down your tempo and try to feel the lightness of the club so that you are *swinging* the grip end rather than forcing it. Try for a loud "swish" sound through the impact area. Then turn the club back over and grip it as you normally do. The clubhead will feel as if it weighs a ton. Swing this "heavy" head a few times with that slower rhythm and you will be amazed at how quickly you can get your timing back.

FEEL THE FORCE

YOU WILL probably be surprised to learn just how little force you need to start your down-swing. For most of you I suspect it would be less force than you think.

Without a club, stand up and extend your arms out to your sides horizontally. Now simply let your arms fall. That's all the force you need to *start* your downswing. Then pour it on!

CHECK YOURSELF IN A MIRROR

A LOT of ranges and teaching centers have mirrors nowadays, or maybe you have a long enough mirror and a high enough ceiling at home. I like to check my positions at address, at the top, and at the finish of my swing in a mirror. Don't worry, you'll get used to seeing a reverse image in the mirror.

Look down at the ball, take your backswing, and stop at the top. Swivel your head to look in the mirror to see if your hands and the club are where you want them at the top, or "in the slot," as I'm showing in this photo.

MASTER THE TRANSITION MOVE

TO WORK on the key transition move from back-swing to downswing, I like this drill. Go to the top of the swing and then *in slow motion* start the hips turning back around before the shoulders and arms move. This is separation. That gives me a sense of the sequence of motions.

Then I will be able to take that timing and enhance it to real swing speed. Ultimately it all must blend into a cohesive, rhythmic swing.

FIND A CONSISTENT SPINE ANGLE

KEEPING THE same spine angle from the start of the swing until past impact is absolutely vital to making consistent contact with the golf ball. Here's a drill I do to check my spine angle. I call it The Coat Hanger Drill. You can do it in your backyard.

Bend the hook of a hanger into a circle, then straighten the wire and stick the other end in the ground. Set up to a ball so that you're looking at it through the circle made by the hook. Don't worry if the ball's not exactly centered.

When you make your backswing, the ball should still show in the circle. When you make your down-swing, it should still be showing in the circle. It's okay if the ball appears to move sideways: If my head shifts somewhat to the right as I swing back, the ball will move to the right of the circle. Just make sure the ball returns to the center of the circle at impact.

It is *not* okay if the ball shifts away from or closer to you, because that means your spine angle is changing. Your head may be bobbing up or down, in or out, which results in erratic contact.

Keep the ball in the circle and your spine angle will remain steady. This simple drill helps promote a shoulder turn that stays on plane and creates more consistent ball contact, which *leads to more accurate shots*: the golfer's Holy Grail!

Watch Tom Watson giving a demonstration of one of the lessons featured within this chapter. Go to http://gettag.mobi for your free mobile app, then point your smartphone's camera at the Microsoft Tag and enjoy the video.

MAKE RIGHT-HAND-ONLY SWINGS

NICK PRICE likes to make practice swings with only his right hand on the club. He does this to reinforce consistent timing in his swing.

Using only the right hand to swing the club makes you feel the weight of the clubhead. The club feels heavier, so you naturally swing a little slower and with more rhythm. The right hand is responsible for releasing the club through impact—and you have to be consistent in that.

Remember: Light grip pressure is essential.

THINK OF A BATTER'S RELEASE

VISUALIZING A baseball slugger's aggressive release can help golfers. Look at this player's right forearm rolling over his left forearm. Swinging a bat is a good golf drill.

RELEASE A BALL

FAILING TO release the clubhead is such a common shortcoming that I'm devoting extra attention to it. It's a good way to cure the slice that afflicts so many of you. This is a fun drill I've used to free up my release. If you've ever played baseball or softball, you can identify with it.

I'm going to throw a ball underhanded with my right hand while my left hand holds the club steady on the ground. I make a regular backswing turn, then turn back through and throw the ball toward my target.

I want to keep my body tilt consistent throughout. This exercise gives you the natural feeling of a full release, without the pressure of hitting a ball.

GET ON THE BALL

TO PREVENT problems with the lower body, I've practiced using a Mickey Wright tip to put a ball under the middle-outside of my right shoe. That keeps my center of gravity on the inside of the right foot, and encourages the right hip to turn back rather than slide over.

Your upper body coils more. Ben Hogan and other players including me have commented that Mickey had one of the best swings we ever saw. I was very impressed by the consistency of her swing plane.

LEARN A GOOD
SHOULDER TURN

HERE'S A simple drill to learn the correct shoulder turn in your golf swing.

1. TAKE your address position and hold a club at each end across your shoulders and the back of your neck. Your right shoulder is slightly lower than your left.

2. MAKE a full backswing shoulder turn. Note where your left hand and the end of the club are pointing.

3. NOW turn your shoulders as you would on the downswing, through impact to the finish. Make your right hand end up in the same place your left hand was at the end of your backswing.

This gives you the proper shoulder rotation in your swing. Practice the shoulder drill slowly at first, then faster. Finally, swing the club normally, feeling the turn you just practiced.

SIMPLY SHAKE HANDS

WE ALL make the golf swing too complicated. My dad always told me the swing is as simple as shaking hands. You shake hands with your right hand on the backswing, then shake hands with your right hand swinging through.

Take your address position, without a club, your upper body bent over and your knees flexed. Now turn to your right and pretend you are shaking someone's hand at waist height. Your right arm is bent, your left knee works inward, your hips turn out of the way. Then do the same thing in reverse the other way. Your right arm extends, your right knee shifts inward, your hips clear.

That's the golf swing in essence.

WARM UP YOUR MIND

PROS PLAY mind games with themselves, and I'm no exception. After I stretch and warm up my body, I start my pre-round practice with a long club—like a long iron—rather than a wedge. I like to start with an easy full swing to work into my rhythm. The 3-iron is about the hardest club in the bag for me to hit, so I hit it first, at a moderate speed.

Why?

If I flub a shot or two, no big deal. It's supposed to be a tough club to hit. But if I hit it dead flush right away, my confidence is higher. I think, "I've got it today!"

Another thing I will always do when I warm up is practice the toughest shot I'll face on the course I'm playing that day, until I hit it the way I want to. An example would be the tee shot at the 12th hole at Augusta.

WATSON MOMENT

My real '82 U.S. Open key

Golf, like life, is a game of ups and downs. One day you have it, the next day you can't find it. After I finally won the U.S. Open in 1982, most of the attention went to my chip-in on the 71st hole. But I actually won it by fixing my backswing Friday after two rounds with my short game saving me.

Coming into the tournament, my long game was in disarray. I was spraying my drives right and left, and hours of practice weren't helping. The only part of my game that was any good was my short game, and that wasn't going to be enough facing Pebble Beach's narrow fairways and gnarly rough. I didn't give myself any chance to win.

Going to the practice tee after my Friday round, fortunately at even par for 36 holes, I knew I couldn't rely on my short game and have any chance of winning. But then, after an hour of hitting the ball everywhere but where I wanted, I made a simple adjustment to my backswing that brought my shotmaking under control.

The new move was to keep my left arm closer to my chest on the takeaway. That led to my left arm ending up in the "slot"—the proper position between my head and shoulder for the left arm and club at the top of the swing. Before, the arm and club had been too upright, sticking up in the air too much and causing a shortened shoulder turn and erratic contact and shots.

Another hour of practicing the new move late Friday confirmed it. I said to Bruce Edwards, my longtime caddie, "I've got it."

On the first tee the next day I was more nervous than usual, not having tested the new move for real and in the most important tournament I had played. My heart was pounding as I thought only about keeping my left arm close to my chest. I hit a perfect tee shot, splitting the first fairway. Walking off the tee, Bruce said, "It's off to the races now!" and it was. The final two rounds I hit the ball the best I had hit it that year, and I won the tournament I'd always wanted to win most. All because of that simple swing change—and that fortunate chip.

→ A TIMELESS SWING

197

UP THE LINE

DOWN THE LINE

FACE **ON**

Watch Tom Watson giving a demonstration of one of the lessons featured within this chapter. Go to http://gettag.mobi for your free mobile app, then point your smartphone's camera at the Microsoft Tag and enjoy the video.

FROM BEHIND

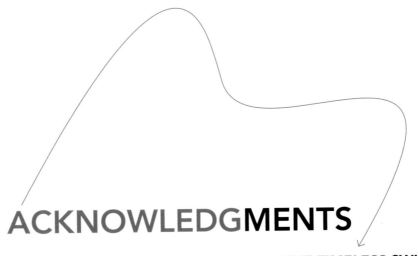

ACKNOWLEDGMENTS

Thanks to all those who helped make possible **THE TIMELESS SWING**

Scott Addison

Peter Borland

Kerry Brady

Steve Breslin

Arnie Brown

J.D. Cuban

Judith Curr

Jeanmarie Ferullo

Kelly Fray

Ariele Fredman

Camille Garmirian

Steve Glassman

Christian Iooss

Walter Iooss Jr.

E. Michael Johnson

Larry Kother

Jeanne Lee

Jim Luft

Bob McGannon

Mary S. Motasky

Paul Olsewski

Larry Pekarek

Vanessa Pierson

Cliff Schrock

Greg Seitz

Nick Simonds

Dana Sloan

Mike Stachura

Stephen Szurlej

Jerry Tarde

Lisa Vannais

Scott Waxman

Guy Yocom

Melissa Yow

WATSON'S TIMELESS RECORD

PROFESSIONAL VICTORIES → 67

MAJOR VICTORIES → 8

MASTERS VICTORIES → 2 (1977, 1981)

U.S. OPEN VICTORIES → 1 (1982, ABOVE)

BRITISH OPEN VICTORIES → 5 (1975, 1977, 1980, 1982, 1983)

CHAMPIONS TOUR VICTORIES → 13 (INCLUDING 5 MAJORS)

PGA PLAYER OF THE YEAR → 6 (1977-1980, 1982, 1984)

PGA TOUR LEADING MONEY WINNER → 5 (1977-1980, 1984)

VARDON TROPHY → 3 (1977-1979)

BOB JONES AWARD → 1 (1987)

OLD TOM MORRIS AWARD → 1 (1992)

PAYNE STEWART AWARD → 1 (2003)

NAMED TO WORLD GOLF HALL OF FAME IN 1988